FOREWORD

This comparative study on the radiological impacts of spent nuclear fuel management options was launched by the OECD Nuclear Energy Agency (NEA) at the request of the OSPAR Commission in 1995. The main objectives of the study were to compile the most recent data and information on radioactive releases from the different stages of two selected nuclear fuel cycles (with and without reprocessing), to analyse radiological impacts in a systematic manner, to interpret the results from the scientific and technological standpoint, and to contribute to informed discussions in NEA Member countries. The study was carried out by the *Ad Hoc* Expert Group on Spent Fuel Management Options under the NEA Committee on Radiation Protection and Public Health. The Expert Group held five meetings between October 1997 and September 1999.

Two simplified reference fuel cycles (with and without reprocessing) based on pressurised-water reactors (PWR) were selected to facilitate the comparison of radiological impacts. Actual data on radioactive releases from reference facilities were used. Reference facilities were selected considering their scale, technological characteristics, duration of operation, characteristics of the installed waste management process, as well as regulatory requirements. Radiological impacts were evaluated with generic models and complemented with results of studies carried out by national and international organisations.

As some operations in the nuclear fuel cycle are still in the process of development, some uncertainties remain. These operations include the reprocessing of mixed-oxide fuel (MOX), the conditioning of spent uranium and MOX fuel for disposal, and the geological disposal of spent fuel and vitrified high-level waste. Given that situation and to the extent that the two reference fuel cycles chosen have several stages in common, efforts were made to apply common assumptions in order to reduce uncertainties.

The study is intended to be generic and limited in scope. While radiological impacts, which are the focus of this study, are important for the decision-making process, it should be noted that certain elements excluded from this study (*e.g.,* resource utilisation efficiency, energy security, economic considerations) should also be considered when making fuel cycle choices.

This study has been financed by voluntary contributions from Belgium, Denmark, Finland, France, Germany, Ireland, Japan, Korea, the Netherlands, Switzerland, the United Kingdom and the European Commission.

The opinions expressed in this report do not necessarily reflect the point of view of NEA Member countries. The report is published on the responsibility of the Secretary-General of the OECD.

TABLE OF CONTENTS

FOREWORD 3

EXECUTIVE SUMMARY 7

1. SCOPE OF THE STUDY 13
1.1 Background 13
1.2 Scope of the Study 13

2. THE PRINCIPLES OF RADIOLOGICAL PROTECTION 17
2.1 Introduction 17
2.2 ICRP Recommendations 17
2.3 National Regulatory Practices 20
2.4 The Environment 20

3. FUEL CYCLE FACILITIES AND RADIOACTIVE DISCHARGES 23
3.1 Uranium Mining and Milling 23
3.2 Conversion, Enrichment and Fuel Fabrication 25
3.3 Power Generation 29
3.4 Interim Storage and Conditioning of Spent Fuel 30
3.5 Reprocessing and Vitrification 32
3.6 Decommissioning and Dismantling of Nuclear Facilities 33
3.7 Disposal of Solid Waste 34
3.8 Transportation 35

4. DOSE ESTIMATION FOR WORKERS 37
4.1 Uranium Mining and Milling 37
4.2 Conversion, Enrichment and Fuel Fabrication 38
4.3 Power Generation 39
4.4 Interim Storage and Conditioning of Spent Fuel 40
4.5 Reprocessing and Vitrification 41
4.6 Decommissioning and Dismantling of Nuclear Facilities 42
4.7 Disposal of Solid Waste 42
4.8 Transportation 42
4.9 Summary of Results and Discussion 45

5. METHODOLOGY FOR GENERIC DOSE ASSESSMENT 47
5.1 Introduction 47
5.2 Radiological Indicators 47
5.3 Methodology for Estimating Doses to Members of the Public from Discharges 48

6.   DOSE ESTIMATION FOR THE PUBLIC 51
6.1 Introduction 51
6.2 Uranium Mining and Milling 51
6.3 Conversion, Enrichment and Fuel Fabrication 53
6.4 Power Generation 53
6.5 Interim Storage and Conditioning 53
6.6 Reprocessing and Vitrification 54
6.7 Disposal of Solid Waste 55
6.8 Summary of Results and Discussion 56

7.   CONCLUSIONS 61

MEMBERS OF THE EXPERT GROUP 65

BIBLIOGRAPHY 66

Annex A – TECHNICAL SITE-SPECIFIC INFORMATION 69
Annex B – GENERIC DOSE ASSESSMENT OF THE NUCLEAR FUEL CYCLE 93
Annex C – GLOSSARY AND CONVERSION FACTORS 121

List of figures

Figure 1.   Reference fuel cycles and fuel flow charts 15
Figure 2.   Trends in the normalised collective occupational dose in French reactors 40

List of tables

Table 1.   Dose limits recommended by the ICRP 19
Table 2.   Generic gaseous release rates from mill tailings, and typical activity concentrations
            in freshwater bodies close to uranium mining and milling facilities 25
Table 3.   Annual discharges from Springfields uranium conversion plant 26
Table 4.   Annual discharges from EURODIF enrichment plant 27
Table 5.   Discharges from the Romans UO_2 fuel fabrication plant 28
Table 6.   Generic discharges from the conversion, enrichment and fuel fabrication stages 28
Table 7.   Annual discharges from FRENCH PWRs 29
Table 8.   Generic annual discharges from a PWR 30
Table 9.   Generic discharges from a reprocessing plant 33
Table 10.   Characteristics of solid waste generation and disposal 35
Table 11.   Occupational exposures in Canadian facilities 37
Table 12   Annual occupational exposures in Australian mines and mills 38
Table 13.   Annual collective occupational doses for the mining and milling stages 38
Table 14.   Trend in occupational doses at the La Hague reprocessing plant 41
Table 15.   Normalised annual collective doses for transport 44
Table 16.   Detailed doses to workers at various fuel-cycle facilities 45
Table 17.   Dose estimation for workers from major fuel-cycle stages of each option 46
Table 18.   Occupancy data 50
Table 19.   Critical group intake data 50
Table 20.   Individual effective doses for specific adult groups
            living close to the La Hague site 55
Table 21.   Dose estimation for the public – Collective dose 56
Table 22.   Dose estimation for the public – Individual dose (critical group) 57
Table 23.   Summary table of dose estimation for the public and workers
            from major fuel cycle stages of each option 61

EXECUTIVE SUMMARY

Objectives and scope

The main objective of this report is to compare the radiological impacts of two spent fuel management options. The reference fuel cycles that have been selected area fuel cycle with reprocessing of spent fuel and one-time recycling of separated plutonium in the form of mixed oxide fuel (MOX) and a once-through fuel cycle where the spent fuel is not reprocessed, but is considered as waste.

The main parameters characterising the two reference fuel cycles are:
- 1 000 MW(e) PWR with approximately 40 GWd/tHM burnup fuel.
- Once-through option:
  - all waste and spent fuel are disposed of in a repository.
- Reprocessing option:
  - all UO_2 spent fuel is reprocessed;
  - all plutonium recovered from reprocessing of UO_2 spent fuel is recycled as MOX fuel only once;
  - all waste, including vitrified high-level waste from reprocessing and MOX spent fuel, is disposed of in a repository.

Several assumptions have been made to facilitate comparison of radiological impacts:
- facilities employ current technology and practices;
- simplified fuel cycles;
- long-term stability of tailings from mining and milling;
- no extensive use of depleted uranium from enrichment, and no reuse of separated uranium from reprocessing; and
- geological disposal of spent fuel from the once-through option, and of vitrified high-level waste and spent MOX fuel from the reprocessing option.

To the extent possible, actual releases and exposure data have been used to represent the state-of-the-art technology and current practices.

The ICRP framework

The comparison of radiological impacts is made within the framework of the recommendations of the International Commission on Radiological Protection (ICRP) as described in its Publication 60 (ICRP 1991). Radiological impacts have been evaluated for members of the general public and for workers, and are presented in terms of critical group doses and collective doses arising from the various stages of the two fuel cycles considered. Collective doses refer to regional populations which, in all cases

7

except for mining and milling, correspond to the population of Europe. Collective doses to the public are summed over 500 years, and are normalised to the electricity produced in gigawatt-years.

There is an ongoing debate within the scientific community regarding the use of collective dose, particularly in the case of small individual doses received by large populations and over many generations into the future (ICRP 1998). Given that no clear consensus has emerged, and that collective dose is used in this report only in a comparative fashion, the Expert Group considered it prudent to base its comparison on the ICRP Publication 60 framework.

The impact on the environment has been considered. Given that there is no consensus at this point on a system of protection specifically for the environment, the Expert Group decided to proceed along ICRP Publication 60 lines.

Generic and site-specific calculations

In calculating doses to members of the public, assumptions had to be made about population distribution, habits of individuals and characteristics of the environment in which they live, and about conditions of releases (meteorological conditions, stack height, etc.). These assumptions can have a considerable influence on the magnitude of calculated doses. This factor introduces difficulties in making a general comparison of radiological impacts of components of the fuel cycle because the impact of a particular nuclear fuel cycle facility will depend to some extent on where the facility is located. Therefore, this study has applied a set of standard assumptions and generic models, in order to compare all stages of the two reference fuel cycles on a common basis. This procedure is referred to as "generic calculation". Site-specific calculations, when available, provide an indication of the sensitivity of the results to these assumptions as well as further insights into the distributions of doses amongst individuals.

It is appropriate to use models to evaluate public doses for several reasons. Doses to the public are very small, and the various contributions of different origin cannot easily be identified and measured directly. The behaviour of radionuclides in the environment is very complex due to many variables, and the same is true for the behaviour of the population in question. In addition, the larger part of doses resulting from a specific discharge will be received much later in the future, when radionuclides have migrated through the environment.

Impact on workers

The occupational doses received over the entire fuel cycle are dominated by doses to workers at the nuclear power plant. The occupational doses to workers in nuclear power plants are not affected by the type of fuel used (UO$_2$ or MOX). At the fuel fabrication stage there is a significant difference between occupational exposures of the two fuel cycle options. However, the absolute values at that stage are only a small fraction of the sum over the whole fuel cycle for both options.

Impact on the public

Generic calculations of impacts on the public have been undertaken by dividing the fuel cycle into four stages: uranium mining and milling, fuel fabrication (including enrichment and uranium conversion), power production, and reprocessing. Results of this study show that the highest radiological impacts come from both the uranium mining/milling and reprocessing stages. Power production gives rise to collective doses that are similar for both options, but lower than those from mining and milling and from reprocessing. Individual does to members of the critical group from power production are very much lower than those from mining and milling or from reprocessing. Fuel fabrication gives rise to the lowest collective doses of any stage.

The assessed collective doses for mining and milling and for reprocessing are similar. This is valid for both the impacts on the general public and on the fuel cycle facility workers. The collective dose summed over 500 years to the regional population (*i.e.*, within a radius of 2 000 km) is up to around 1 manSv/GWa for uranium mining and milling and a maximum of about 1.2 manSv/GWa for reprocessing. Available site-specific calculations support the conclusions of the generic calculations in the sense that the assessed collective dose of an actual reprocessing facility is 0.6 manSv/GWa, and that the critical group doses are higher than for the other two stages (*i.e.*, power plant operation and fuel fabrication) of the fuel cycle that were considered.

For both the uranium mining and milling and the reprocessing stages, the assessed critical group doses are in the range of 0.30 to 0.50 mSv/a. Actual critical group doses at specific sites can be significantly different, due to differences in the habits and location of local populations, etc. However, the results show that in general the potential for exposure of local individuals is similar for these two stages of the fuel cycle.

Based on extensive available data one can conclude that the introduction of MOX fuel in PWRs has not had any noticeable effect on liquid and gaseous releases from reactors during normal operation. Consequently, the radiological impact of the power production stage is the same for both options.

Uncertainties

The uncertainties associated with public-exposure estimates are large. They are associated with the models and scenarios as well as with the underlying parameter values. In particular, uranium mining is very site-specific and doses are strongly influenced by demographic parameters; environmental conditions, characteristics of the uranium-bearing rock, mining and milling practices, long-term stability of disposed tailings, as well as procedures for maintenance and remedial actions. Actual ^{222}Rn emanation rates could be significantly different from those assumed in this study, leading to higher or lower collective doses. Indeed, if the tailing piles were partially uncovered following a period of poor maintenance, collective doses of up to a few tens of mansieverts per gigawatt-year would be possible.

Time frame for the calculation of collective doses

Collective doses to members of the public require critical examination. Collective doses have been calculated to 500 years into the future. It is possible to calculate these doses for longer time periods, including infinity. As collective doses from major components of the fuel cycles (mining and milling, power production and reprocessing) involve long-lived radionuclides, such an approach would lead to larger collective doses. However, calculating the collective dose for longer periods is unlikely to affect the conclusions of the report. The majority of the collective dose calculated for a 500-year period for both power production and reprocessing arises from the relatively long-lived, mobile radionuclide ^{14}C (half-life 5 730 years). Thus extension of the time period considered is not likely to alter the ratio of the impacts of these two processes. For the mining and milling stage, the production of ^{222}Rn in tailings will continue at a slowly declining rate for a period of hundreds of thousands of years because it is generated by the decay of very-long-lived radionuclide ^{230}Th (half-life 77 000 years). While the contribution to the collective doses from this part of the fuel cycle could be considerable if calculated for very long time periods, and could even become the dominant fraction, the ratio of collective doses from the two options would not change significantly. For these reasons, and because of the large uncertainties associated with scenarios in the far future, longer periods have not been considered in the study.

Mining and milling reduction *versus* reprocessing

The mining and milling, power production and reprocessing stages dominate the collective doses to the public. While power production causes the same radiological impacts for both fuel cycle options, the variations in the radiological impacts of the other two stages tend to be in opposite directions. Through reprocessing and through the use of MOX-fuel, the need for natural uranium could be reduced by about 21%, and consequently the public and worker exposures caused by the mining and milling stage should be reduced in the same proportion. On the other hand, the reprocessing stage adds to the public and worker collective doses. However, it should not be forgotten that the assessed public collective doses, and the overall radiological comparison of options, are highly sensitive to assumptions regarding good mill-tailing pile management.

Important nuclides

Only a few radionuclides are important for the purposes of this report. The main contributor to the total collective dose for power production is ^{14}C. For reprocessing, ^{14}C again, with ^{129}I and ^{85}Kr, is mainly responsible for radiological impacts. These radionuclides, discharged at levels in compliance with regulations, disperse in the environment but are at levels that can still be measured with modern technology. They constitute a potential source of very low doses to the population on a global scale.

The main sources of exposure from the uranium mining and milling stage are daughter nuclides of the naturally occurring uranium decay chains. These represent another potential source in the long-term and on a regional scale.

Disposal of solid waste

In the very long term, radionuclides from an underground repository for HLW or spent fuel could also become a potential source of exposure. Model calculations show that only after several hundreds of thousands of years, a small radiological impact may occur, which is related to ^{129}I, ^{135}Cs or ^{99}Tc depending on the characteristics of the repository. Collective doses are composed of very small individual doses to a large number of people over a long period of time. Because these doses are small and are expected to be similar for both fuel cycles considered in the study, they have not been included in the comparative analysis.

Transportation

Regarding both the public and occupational exposures caused by transportation, it has not been possible to make any clear difference between the two options, although the types of material trans-ported and distances involved are somewhat different. Nevertheless, the radiological impact caused by transportation is small compared to the total impact and to the dominant stages of the fuel cycle.

Conclusions

The differences between the two fuel cycles examined in the report are small from the standpoint of radiological impact. Taking into account limitations inherent in the generic calculations, it is simply not justifiable to draw definitive conclusions from the small differences in collective and individual radiological impacts. Consequently, radiological impact is not a key factor favouring one option or the other. Rather, other factors such as resource utilisation efficiency, energy security, and economics would tend to carry more weight in the decision-making process. Overall, the public exposures in both options are low compared to the pertinent regulatory limits, and also insignificantly low compared with exposures from natural background radiation (the world wide average annual individual dose from natural radiation is 2.4 mSv).

Trends

Doses to workers at nuclear installations have been reduced in recent years. There has also been a diminishing trend in discharges from all stages of the nuclear fuel cycle achieved on the basis of feedback from operating experience and the application of new technology and improved procedures. This trend is particularly noteworthy in the case of reprocessing plants.

It is probably possible to reduce releases further from reprocessing facilities. Moreover, adequate remedial actions exist to reduce long-term radiological impacts caused by radon exhalation from mining and milling tailing piles to insignificant levels after operation. However it seems difficult to reduce further the radon release during the operating phase of mining and milling.

Need for further studies

For the purpose of this report, decisions have been made regarding the use of collective dose to compare radiological impacts, the management of depleted and separated uranium, the management of MOX fuel, the long-term safety assessment of geological disposal, etc. This methodology may need to be re-evaluated in the future in the light of developments such as new environmental transfer models, changes affecting the system of radiation protection (including the use of collective dose), new impact indicators for the environment, etc.

A comprehensive comparison of the two spent fuel management options would necessarily involve a broad range of other issues, in addition to radiological impact, raised by the normal operation of fuel cycle facilities. These would include issues noted in the conclusions above to include environmental protection, waste management, resource utilisation efficiency, energy security and economics. In the plant-specific regulatory process, the consideration of incidents and other abnormal events is required. These other aspects are not addressed in this report since they are outside its scope. It is anticipated, however, that this report will serve as a basis of broader studies on nuclear power development strategy, nuclear fuel cycle strategy and sustainable development of nuclear power.

1. SCOPE OF THE STUDY

1.1 Background

The Steering Committee of the Nuclear Energy Agency decided in 1995 to launch, at the request of the Oslo and Paris Commissions (OSPAR) a comparative study of the radiological impacts of spent fuel management options in 1995. The original request was centred on comparative assessment of radiological impacts from radioactive discharges into the marine environment resulting from reprocessing and once-through options. In deciding to launch the study, the Steering Committee took account of recommendations of the Committee on Radiation Protection and Public Health (CRPPH) that a narrow scope for such a study would be of limited interest, from radiation protection view point, and that the study's scope should cover all stages in the fuel cycle.

It was thus agreed that the main purposes of the study would be:

- to compile scientific and technological data and information relevant to the request; and

- to analyse these data and present findings with scientific and technological interpretations to assist discussions by the OSPAR Member countries.

The CRPPH recommended, for purpose of efficiency, to rely as much as possible on existing information. Consequently, published site-specific data have been extensively used. Nevertheless, a series of calculations, performed by the National Radiological Protection Board (NRPB), has been necessary to allow data of different origins to be comparable. Results of previous similar studies have also been considered and used as appropriate. These studies include the IAEA International Nuclear Fuel Cycle Evaluation (INFCE) (IAEA 1980), the European Commission Project's ExternE–Externalities of Energy (EUR 1995), and the 1983 German comparison of the safety of reprocessing and once-through options and its updated version in 1996 (Hörmann 1996).

1.2 Scope of the Study

Evaluation of radiological impacts is complex due to the influence of a number of factors: plant characteristics, regulatory requirements, operating conditions, site characteristics, environmental aspects, cultural and social conditions. Specifically, this study attempts to present a systematic comparison of radiological impacts arising from reprocessing and once-through options. The stylised fuel cycles chosen for this study are somewhat different from actual fuel cycles, thus the numerical results should not be interpreted in an absolute sense. However, the stylised fuel cycles used for this study are comprehensive, and are sufficiently detailed for realistic comparison purposes (see Figure 1). The following equivalent parameters and conditions are used for the study:

- 1 000 MW(e) PWR, with 40 GWd/tHM burnup fuel.

- Once-through option:
  - all waste and spent fuel are disposed of into a repository.

- Reprocessing option:
  - all uranium-dioxide (UO_2) spent fuel is reprocessed;
  - all plutonium recovered from reprocessing of UO_2 spent fuel is recycled as MOX fuel only once;
  - no reuse of separated uranium from reprocessing;
  - all waste and MOX spent fuel are disposed of into a repository.

It is emphasised that the study is based on current technology and current practices in selected facilities of the nuclear fuel cycle. The current internationally accepted system of radiation protection, described in Chapter 2, forms the basis for the analyses of radiological impacts.

Only normal operation has been considered. The analysis of accidents was considered to be outside the scope of this study.

The amount of electricity produced has been chosen as the common basis for comparison for this study. Releases and discharges into the marine environment and the atmosphere have consequently been normalised to one unit (1 GWa) of electricity produced. It should be noted, however, that in real situations, discharges, releases and doses are not correlated uniquely with the electricity production. For example worker doses also depend on the design, on the age of the plant, and on the amount of maintenance work performed.

In evaluating radiological impacts, a generic model and common parameters are used to facilitate systematic comparison of results. Actual radioactive release data of plants with state-of-the-art characteristics are used as much as possible so that the results reflect current practices. When actual releases are not available, the needed information is derived from evaluation of the literature. Detailed descriptions of releases from each stage of the fuel cycle considered are presented in Chapter 3. Results are presented in terms of the activity released, expressed in gigabecquerels (GBq).

Radiological impacts are evaluated in terms of individual doses and collective doses. Emphasis is placed on doses to the public, but doses to workers are also presented. A short review of the radiological impacts on the environment, based mostly on previously published reviews by other international organisations, is also included in the report. As in other similar studies, the comparison of the defined spent fuel management options is mainly based on calculated collective doses, truncated at 500 years. This is compatible with the *1990 Recommendations of the International Commission on Radiological Protection*, Publication 60 (ICRP 1991) as discussed in Chapters 2 and 5.

Reprocessing and plutonium recycling allow the production of more energy from the same initial quantity of mined uranium. Expressed from a different point of view, the same amount of energy can be produced with less mining and milling activity if plutonium is recycled. Fuel amounts provided in Figure 1 are normalised to energy production. The fuel flow chart of the once-through option shows that the production of 1 GWa requires the mining and milling of 179.3 t of natural uranium. The flow chart for the reprocessing option shows that this quantity can be reduced to 141.7 t when plutonium, recovered by reprocessing, is recycled in the production of MOX fuel.

The reference fuel management options of Figure 1 do not present complete cycles. In both cases, depleted uranium (normally stored temporarily as hexafluoride) requires additional steps, either for further use (*e.g.,* for further enrichment) or for eventual disposal after conditioning. Uranium separated by reprocessing may be and has been used for re-enrichment and as fuel in reactors, although the impacts of such uses have not been included in this study.

14

Figure 1.   Reference fuel cycles and fuel flow charts adopted for the study
(Adapted from Hörmann 1996)

Once-through Option

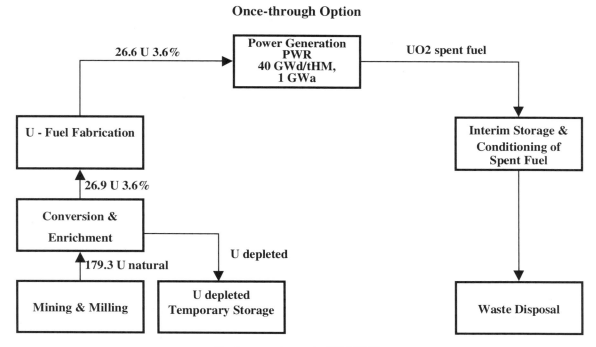

Fuel amounts are in tHM/GWa

Reprocessing Option

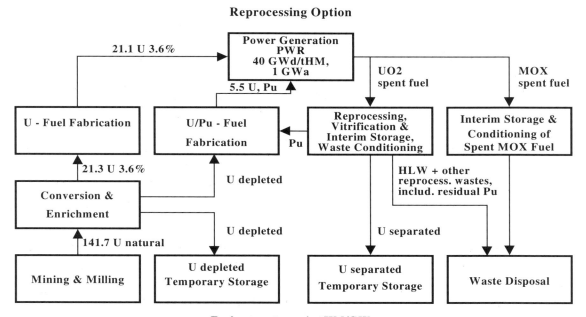

Fuel amounts are in tHM/GWa

2. THE PRINCIPLES OF RADIOLOGICAL PROTECTION

2.1   Introduction

Ionising radiation can cause health effects. At the doses of interest in this report, induction of fatal cancer is the health effect of most concern. Recommendations for the protection of people from the harmful effects of ionising radiation are made by the International Commission on Radiological Protection (ICRP). The Commission is a non-governmental body of experts. ICRP's latest recommendations for a system of radiological protection were published as ICRP Publication 60 in 1991 (ICRP 1991). Competent national regulatory authorities have developed regulatory systems that generally follow the broad lines of ICRP recommendations.

The study presented in this report is based on ICRP 60 recommendations, and quantities recommended by ICRP are used, although discussions are going on worldwide concerning the applicability of the basic approaches and assumptions. Reservations have been expressed in particular regarding:

(i)   the extents to which radiological protection should rely on the concept of a linear, no-threshold dose response relationship; and

(ii) the concept of collective dose, especially when applied to the summation of a very large number of very small doses over long time periods.

The interest of using the collective dose concept lies in convenience as a practical tool to compare the two options on dosimetric grounds. However the authors are well aware of the limitations and potential shortcomings of its use, particularly the large uncertainties associated with its interpretation in absolute rather than relative terms. At the low individual doses postulated in this study there are large uncertainties associated with the extrapolation from dose to the risk of health detriments. While these uncertainties are of less concern when collective doses are used in a comparative fashion, the validity of their use as an absolute measure of detriment is questionable.

A detailed consideration of the basic principles of radiation protection and the description of the state of the art in that field fall beyond the scope and main purpose of this report. However, a summary of the main characteristics of the system of radiation protection will provide useful background.

2.2   ICRP Recommendations

The primary aim of radiological protection, as stated by ICRP, is to provide an appropriate standard of protection for mankind without unduly limiting the beneficial practices giving rise to the radiation exposure. Given the great scientific uncertainties in the assessment of risk, particularly at low doses, this aim has been applied to recommendations and regulations in a precautionary fashion through the use of a linear no-threshold assumption. This assumption underlies ICRP recommendations, and states that for small increases in dose above the dose from natural radiation sources, the increment in risk is proportional to the increment in dose with no threshold. Thus, standards and recommendations are based on limiting by all reasonable means the risk of health effects, but not on eliminating that risk entirely. Whether or not there are health effects at low radiation doses is difficult to establish and is, to some extent at least, controversial.

The recommendations made by ICRP form a basis for the European Basic Safety Standards (EC, 1996), which are mandatory within the European Union, and for the International Basic Safety Standards which are issued under the auspices of a number of international agencies, primarily the International Atomic Energy Agency (IAEA 1996).

There are two categories of radiation dose. The first category is the dose to an individual[1]. The unit of radiation dose is the sievert (Sv). This is a large unit and doses are usually reported in millisieverts (one thousandth of a sievert – mSv), or microsieverts (one millionth of a sievert – µSv). From the "linear-no-threshold" assumption, the health risk to an individual from ionising radiation is directly proportional to the dose. The second category is the sum of the doses to all the individuals in an exposed population. This is called the collective dose; the unit of collective dose is the man-sievert (manSv). It can be shown from the linear no-threshold assumption that the number of delayed radiation-induced health effects (in this context, usually the number of fatal cancers) in an exposed population is in proportion to the collective dose.

Evaluating the collective dose to the workers is relatively straightforward. However, particular problems can arise concerning both the estimation of collective doses to members of the public and their meaning. One issue is that a collective dose to an exposed population of members of the public is often the result of the summation of very small individual doses to very large numbers of people. As only normal operation is considered in this study, the resulting individual doses, especially to the population, are very low and far below the annual doses from natural radiation (the world wide average annual individual dose from natural radiation is 2.4 mSv, UNSCEAR 1996). In addition, the calculation of collective doses is rather sensitive to the variation of assumptions and to the definition of population characteristics and time frames.

The system of radiological protection distinguishes two broad categories of situations: practices and interventions. Practices are human activities that add doses to those people already receiving. Industries discharging radionuclides to the environment are practices as the discharges cause doses to some individuals over and above those that they would normally incur from natural radiation. A distinguishing feature of practices is that they are undertaken as a matter of choice for some beneficial reason. The benefit should be sufficient to offset not only the costs and other inconveniences caused by the operation of the practice, but also of the detriment from the attributable radiation exposure. Steps taken to control doses from practices are planned in advance and are applied to the source of the exposure. Interventions are human activities that reduce the doses that people are receiving, or are likely to receive, from existing situations, the presence of which is not a matter of choice. Intervention reduces doses from situations that are regarded as unsatisfactory from a radiological protection viewpoint. The generation of electricity using nuclear power is a practice and the system of protection for practices applies. Therefore, the remainder of this section focuses on this system.

The system of radiological protection recommended by ICRP for proposed and continuing practices has the following principles:

(i) No practice involving exposures to radiation should be adopted unless it produces sufficient benefit to the exposed individuals or to society to offset the radiation detriment it causes (the justification of a practice). The decision regarding whether a practice should be considered justified is likely to invoke factors that go far beyond radiological protection.

---

1. In this report, the term "dose" refers to effective dose as defined in ICRP Publication 60.

(ii) In relation to any particular source within a practice, the magnitude of individual doses, the number of people exposed, and the likelihood of incurring exposures where these are not certain to be received should all be kept as low as reasonably achievable, economic and social factors being taken into account. This procedure should be constrained by restrictions on the doses to individuals (dose constraints), or the risks to individuals in the case of potential exposures (risk constraints), so as to limit the inequity likely to result from the inherent economic and social judgements. (The optimisation of protection.)

(iii) The exposure of individuals resulting from the combination of all the relevant practices should be subject to dose limits, or to some control of risk in the case of potential exposures. These are aimed at ensuring that no individual is exposed to radiation risks that are judged to be unacceptable from these practices in any normal circumstances. (Individual dose and risk limits.)

Occupational exposures are those incurred at work as the result of situations that can reasonably be regarded as the responsibility of the operating management. Public exposure encompasses all exposures other than occupational and medical from sources under regulatory control. Occupational and public exposures are relevant to this report.

The process of optimisation of protection is broadly intended to ensure that the resources expended in reducing radiation detriment, *i.e.*, in reducing individual and collective doses, are not disproportionate to the benefits gained. In optimising protection it is important that all relevant aspects of radiation detriment are considered. For example, one option for the management of liquid radioactive wastes might be treatment to extract some fraction of the radionuclide content prior to release to the environment. The extracted radionuclides will require storing and eventually, disposal, and the doses to workers and members of the public from these operations will be factors in the optimisation decision. There are various procedures available for optimisation of protection. Many of these procedures involve comparing reductions in the numbers of health effects in the exposed population with the resources required in order to achieve that reduction. Radiological protection is optimised when the next step in reducing the health effects can only be achieved by a seriously disproportionate use of resources.

The remaining principle is compliance with dose limits. There are different limits for members of the public and for workers. The principal dose limit for members of the public is 1 mSv in a year. The limit applies to the total dose from all sources, subject to control through the system of protection for practices: medical exposures and exposures to natural radiation are excluded. For occupational exposure, ICRP recommends a dose limit of 20 mSv/a averaged over five years, with the further provision that the effective dose should not exceed 50 mSv in any single year. These limits apply to the sum of the exposures incurred at work as a result of situations that can reasonably be regarded as the responsibility of the operating management. In the case of both public and occupational exposure, there are additional limits on doses to the lens of the eye and the skin and, in the case of occupational exposure only, on the doses to the hands and feet. A summary of the relevant internationally recommended dose limits is given in Table 1.

Table 1. **Dose limits recommended by the ICRP**

Application	Dose limits	
	Occupational	**Public**
Effective dose	20 mSv/a, averaged over defined periods of 5 years	1 mSv in a year

International recommendations and standards place limits on doses to individuals; there are no corresponding criteria for collective doses. The main use of the quantity collective dose is in comparing different sources of radioactivity, and for different radiation protection options, during the process of optimisation of radiological protection.

In applying limits, it is not practicable to assess doses to each individual member of the public. The critical group approach is used in order to arrive at an estimate of the likely dose to the most exposed individual. A critical group is a group of members of the public who, by virtue of location and habits, is expected to receive the highest doses from the source in question. The group is usually relatively small in size and usually comprises a few to a few tens of individuals; the average individual dose in the group is compared with the constraint or limit.

In comparing options for the management of radioactive wastes, it is important to recognise that it is the differences between the options that should form the basis for comparison. However, comparisons can be truncated at the point where the uncertainties obscure differences between the options.

When making comparisons based on collective dose, the ICRP has recommended some prudence, particularly when doses are projected into the far future. Specifically, ICRP Publication 77 states that:

> The problems of estimating collective dose over long periods of time are those of uncertainty. Both the individual doses and the size of the exposed populations become increasingly uncertain as the time increases. Furthermore, the current judgements about the relationship between dose and detriment may not be valid for future populations. No detailed guidance can be given, because some situations can be forecast with confidence further into the future than can others. Decisions must be made on a case-by-case basis. In general, however, forecasts of collective dose over periods longer than several thousand years and forecasts of health detriment over periods longer than several hundred years should be critically examined (ICRP 1998).

2.3   National Regulatory Practices

In accordance with national regulation, operators will apply for construction permits and operating licenses with detailed safety assessment reports. These reports usually contain detailed descriptions of site and plant characteristics, operating conditions, estimated radioactive release, estimated radiological impacts, models used to evaluate the impacts and measures to comply with the regulatory requirements.

The competent regulatory authorities review the operator's safety assessment report and issue permit or license. Whenever necessary, the authorities may attach specific conditions to the permit or license.

When the plant subsequently begins operation, the operator shall comply with regulatory requirements and implement its own monitoring programme to ensure that the plant is operated within the requirements. Local or national competent bodies also implement independent monitoring programme.

2.4   The Environment

The need to allow specifically for the potential impact of ionising radiation on the environment as a result of releases of radioactive wastes into it has, for a long time, been subsumed into statements made by the ICRP. In its Publication 26 (ICRP 1977), the Commission stated that:

> Although the principal objective of radiation protection is the achievement and maintenance of appropriately safe conditions for activities involving human exposure, the level of safety required for the protection of all human individuals is thought likely to be adequate to protect other species, although not necessarily individual members of those species. The Commission therefore believes that if man is adequately protected then other living things are also likely to be sufficiently protected.

More recently (ICRP 1991) the Commission has stated that, although its environmental interests are solely concerned with the transfer of radionuclides through the environment, since this directly affects the radiological protection of man, nevertheless:

> The Commission believes that the standard of environmental control needed to protect man to the degree currently thought desirable will ensure that other species are not put at risk. Occasionally, individual members of non-human species might be harmed, but not to the extent of endangering whole species or creating imbalance between species.

Much of the current emphasis behind environmental protection in the case of *non-radioactive* pollutants is based on the premise that, in order to protect and sustain the human species, it is first necessary to protect the environment. It has been pointed out that this is the opposite of the framework used for radiological protection, and that there has never been an internationally agreed set of criteria for the protection of the natural environment from the effects of ionising radiation (Pentreath 1998). Some of the criteria that might be considered within an overall theoretical framework, what is still required to achieve them, and what the practical implications are from a regulatory perspective, have recently been explored (Pentreath 1998; Pentreath 1999; Woodhead 1998).

A review published by the IAEA (IAEA 1992) concluded that there was, at that stage, no convincing evidence from the scientific literature that chronic radiation dose rates below 1 milli-gray/day (mGy/d) would harm animal or plant populations, and that it was highly probable that limitation of the exposure of the most exposed humans (the critical group) living on and receiving full sustenance from the local area, to 1 mSv/a would lead to dose rates to plants and animals in the same area of less than 1 mGy/d.[1]

More recently, from extensive reviews of the available data, it has been concluded (UNSCEAR 1996, Woodhead 1998) that under continuing lifetime irradiation there are unlikely to be any significant effects in wild populations of either terrestrial plants and aquatic organisms (freshwater, coastal marine and deep ocean) at absorbed dose rates less than 400 µGy/h, or of terrestrial animals at absorbed dose rates less than 40 µGy/h, from all sources. In each case, the limiting dose rates from the contamination relate to the most highly exposed individuals in the populations, in the expectation that the mean dose rates across the populations would be lower in a majority of situations. There is also the qualification that the limiting dose rates relate to exposures from low LET radiation.

Further consideration is currently being given to this subject internationally, in particular through the activities of the ICRP and the IAEA (*e.g.,* IAEA 1999). It must be recognised, however, that any framework and criteria specifically for the protection of the environment from ionising radiation are currently at the stage of development rather than implementation. In these circumstances, the basis of the present document remains that of ICRP 60 (1991) quoted above.

---

1. In terms of units, one should note that it is generally not appropriate to use the sievert for species other than humans, and that the gray (Gy) should be used.

3. FUEL CYCLE FACILITIES AND RADIOACTIVE DISCHARGES

3.1 Uranium Mining and Milling

Wherever possible, data from facilities in Western Europe were taken as these data are generally comprehensive and of direct relevance to the scope of the study. The exception is uranium mining and milling for which there was not an appropriate site in Western Europe.

Uranium is the fuel used in nearly all existing nuclear reactors. It is present in the earth's crust at low average concentrations of about 1 to 4 ppm (part per million by weight), but may be concentrated in mineral deposits up to a few percent, occasionally even higher.

Uranium may occur as the predominant metallic constituent (monometallic deposits) or may be accompanied by other metals, particularly nickel, cobalt and arsenic (polymetallic deposits). As a primary product, uranium-bearing ores are generally exploitable at concentrations in excess of several hundred parts per million while as a by-product, uranium can be economically extracted at concentrations around 100 parts per million or less.

Mining of uranium ores is commonly carried out by either underground or open pit techniques. Compared to underground mining, the amount of waste material is larger for open pit methods due to the relatively large volumes involved. A third milling method, in-situ leaching finds more limited application (13% of worldwide uranium production), owing to the specific prerequisites for this type of process. In open-pit and underground mining, uranium is extracted from the crushed ore in a processing plant (mill) using chemical methods appropriate to the specific mineral form. The concentrated form of uranium produced in the plant is called uranium oxide (U_3O_8), and contains 0.7% of the fissile isotope ^{235}U. Depending on its quality, the concentrate is sometimes further purified in a refinery near the mill before being shipped to a conversion plant.

The radioactivity of the separated uranium is very low. The radioactive daughter products, with ^{230}Th as the dominant long-lived radionuclide (half-life of 77 000 years), are left with the mill tailings. They may also contain stable toxic elements such as arsenic, nickel etc. After stabilisation and other technical remedial actions, the tailings are stored adjacent to the mining area in purpose built dams, mined out pits or ring-dike impoundments.

Releases from specific facilities

During mining and milling, particles and radioactive gases are continuously released to air and to water in very small quantities. Ventilation to reduce exposures from inhaled radionuclides and radiological protection measures against external irradiation are critical parts of any mining operation, in particular with underground mines. The run-off water of mills may contain radionuclides and requires rigorous management. It is usually contained on-site or only discharged after treatment. Seepage from the tailings and waste rock may transport dissolved radionuclides into the ground water. In addition, dried tailings may give rise to airborne dispersion of contaminated dust, and surface waters may become contaminated thereby indirectly giving rise to airborne dispersion.

The stored tailings may constitute a source of radon for a long time period. Radon emanation rates from tailings vary considerably depending on the ore grade of the tailings source material, the characteristics of the storage facility and the rehabilitation program. Since storage facilities are normally kept moist and covered, thus the hazards are low.

The releases from the mining and milling processes do not generally occur from a well-defined and monitored point source, thus making the definition of a source term complicated. The mining and milling operations are spread over large areas. Although dusts and gases are released from stacks used to vent the underground tunnels, and particles released from more "closed" facilities may be controlled through filtration, the control of releases is not generally applicable to open pit mining. This reinforces the need for appropriate management practices at mining milling sites to minimise dust and gas release.

In the UNSCEAR Report 1993, the radon exhalation rate from bare tailings is assumed to range between 10 and 300 Bq m^{-2} s^{-1}. After the active surveillance period the applied remedial actions are assumed to restrict the average radon release rate to the level of 3 Bq m^{-2} s^{-1}.

In a recent study by SENES Consultants (SENES 1998), information was gathered from eight major uranium production facilities on future releases of radon from their tailings after remediation. In the report, the mean radon release rate for those sites was estimated to range from 0 to 7 Bq m^{-2} s^{-1}.

Other radionuclides in the decay series that are of potential importance in view of abandoned mill tailings, are ^{210}Pb and ^{210}Po. These radionuclides may accumulate in the vicinity of the mine and through the food chain cause radiation doses to man. Possible leaching of ^{226}Ra into the ground water is another example of a potential critical pathway, giving rise to exposures in the far future.

The environment around the mines usually exhibits high natural background of radioactivity due to the uranium in the ore, which makes it difficult to distinguish the releases and the exposures, caused by the mining, from the background.

Reference mining and milling facility and generic discharges

Data for the generic calculations were taken from the UNSCEAR Report 1993 and from four modern uranium mining and milling facilities, Key Lake and Cluff Lake mines in Canada, and Ranger and Olympic Dam mines in Australia. On the basis of these data it was assumed that the uranium tailings occupied an area of 100 ha and released ^{222}Rn at an initial average rate of 3 Bq m^{-2} s^{-1}. Releases could continue at this rate for many years, nevertheless, during operation layers of tailings materials are put on the top of each other and thus the exhalation rate of the previous layer is reduced. Gradually some countermeasures are implemented and after the operational time effective remedial actions (solid or water material cover) are taken to reduce the radon releases practically to zero.

For the study, releases of ^{222}Rn were normalised to 1 GWa of electricity on the basis that the corresponding tailings cover 1 ha (UNSCEAR 1993). It was further assumed that the tailings arising from uranium production for 1 GWa will eventually be covered by other tailings and the heap would eventually be capped by an inert layer of material reducing radon emissions to zero. Thus, it looked reasonable to assume that the tailings associated with 1 GWa of electricity production would release ^{222}Rn for a period of 10 to 15 years.

The possibility of protracted releases due to poor maintenance of the tailings cannot be entirely discounted and it is possible that releases may increase by several orders of magnitude over long time storage. The uncertainty associated with post operational phase releases is crucial to the study and therefore deserves a comprehensive discussion. The SENES report suggested (from proposed rehabili-tation plans) a radon release rate of zero for Key Lake and Ranger, about 0.2 Bq m^{-2} s^{-1} for Olympic

Dam, and 7 Bq m^{-2} s^{-1} for Cluff Lake after closure and decommissioning. Based on today's experience, absolute "zero" releases from mill tailings after decommissioning is questionable. However, for surface tailings with good compact cover the expected rate will be low, although there is a possibility that some dust or radon may be released for several years. Experience from Rabbit Lake (sub-gaseous deposition) open pit has shown that the releases are so low that they cannot be detected. For in-pit tailings management area with a waste rock cover and a water cover the expected radon release will also be very low and likely not measurable from background within 0.5 km of the pit. Conventional understanding is that a reasonable water cover (see Annex A) over tailings will delay radon movement to the extent that the radon will decay before it can reach the atmosphere. Soil cover will not be as effective resulting in an attenuated exhalation of radon depending on the cover thickness, permeability and saturation.

Finally, one could expect that covering of tailings would presumably follow "good practice" and that the technique used would be modern. Therefore, the assumption of an operational period of 15 years and then decommissioning of the mine with zero release during 500 years seems reasonable.

Tailings may also release radionuclides by leaching into water bodies. Typical concentrations of radionuclides in water bodies close to uranium mining and milling facilities are given in Table 2. They are based on Canadian data (AECB information).

Table 2.   **Generic gaseous release rates from mill tailings, and typical activity concentrations in freshwater bodies close to uranium mining and milling facilities**

Radionuclide	Release rate for gaseous discharges from mill tailings[1] (Bq m^{-2} s^{-1})	Radionuclide concentrations in freshwater bodies[2] (Bq L^{-1})
^{222}Rn	3	
^{226}Ra		0.05
^{210}Pb		0.05
^{210}Po		0.05

1. Tailings of the generic facility are assumed to occupy 100 ha, and the annual release at this rate corresponds to approximately 9.5×10^4 GBq/a. Tailings corresponding to a production of 1 GWa, however, only cover 1 ha, hence a scaling factor of 100 is used in Chapter 6 to calculate collective doses to members of the public.
2. These data represent actual measurements, which include both natural background levels and radionuclides resulting from mining and milling activities.

3.2   Conversion, Enrichment and Fuel Fabrication

Uranium ore concentrate to uranium hexafluoride conversion

The uranium-ore concentrate (UOC) coming from mining and milling is converted to uranium hexafluoride (UF$_6$), which is solid at room temperature thus suitable for storage and transportation, to feed the enrichment process. The ore concentrate is purified through filtration and solvent extraction processes. Purified uranium compound undergoes several chemical processes leading to UF$_6$, which is stored in solid form in condenser vessels.

Filtration and solvent extraction processes are the main sources of radioactive discharges from a conversion facility. The filtration process produces filter cakes containing the insoluble impurities containing a trace amount of uranium and other radioactive nuclides. The filter cakes are sent for disposal in accordance with national regulations. The solvent extraction process produces raffinate effluent containing trace amount of uranium and other radioactive nuclides. The effluent is neutralised and discharged in accordance with regulations.

There are several UF_6 conversion plants in operation in the NEA area. BNFL Springfields, UK, where UF_6 conversion is, among other activities, performed, is selected as a reference facility since comprehensive release data are available. The majority of liquid radioactivity discharged from the Springfields site originates from the conversion of UOC to UF_6, so, it is a maximising assumption to take the total site discharge data as representing the UOC to UF_6 process. For gaseous releases, the UF_6 conversion facility does not make up a large percentage of the Springfields site liquid releases: data from these plants show that they discharged (principally as natural uranium alpha activity) approximately 0.7 GBq in 1995, 0.7 GBq in 1996 and 0.3 GBq in 1997. The releases from Malvesi and Pierrelatte, France, are similar (see Annex A).

Table 3. **Annual discharges from Springfields uranium conversion plant**
(1997 annual throughput: 7 000 tUO_2)

Nuclide	Annual discharges (GBq/a)	
	Gaseous	Liquid
^{230}Th	Not discharged	5.2×10^1
^{232}Th	Not discharged	1.1
^{234}Th*	Not discharged	7.2×10^4
^{234m}Pa*	Not discharged	7.2×10^4
^{234}U	5.7×10^{-1}	5.5×10^1

* Based on discharge data for total beta, assumed to consist of 50% ^{234}Th and 50% ^{234m}Pa.

Normalisation, for electricity production, of releases from the conversion, enrichment and fuel fabrication stages is only performed for the generic case.

Uranium enrichment

Two main routes for uranium enrichment, both processing UF_6, have been in widespread use for many years: the gaseous diffusion process and the enrichment by gas centrifuges. Both technologies are proven technically sound and safe stages within the nuclear fuel cycle. Operational experience has been good with low occupational doses and very small discharges of radioactive substances to the environment. The main hazard from enrichment facilities, especially for the workers, is the accidental release of chemically toxic UF_6. Therefore, the prevention of UF_6 leaks and the protection of the workforce from toxic effects of UF_6 and its decomposition products are of paramount importance.

The EURODIF gaseous diffusion enrichment plant at Tricastin, France, is taken as the reference facility for this study because from this large facility real industrial experience is available for many years. As reference plant for the centrifuge enrichment technique, the URENCO enrichment facility at Gronau, Germany, has been selected for similar reasons.

The depleted uranium separated at enrichment process is stored temporarily. A small quantity is presently used for MOX fabrication in some countries. Conversion of depleted UF_6 into a stable chemical form is considered in some countries to facilitate its eventual disposal.

Very small quantities of uranium are vented from the process and auxiliary systems of gaseous diffusion plants to atmosphere. Atmospheric releases from EURODIF in 1997 were 3.3 kgU with a total alpha activity of 0.16 GBq. Discharges in liquid form occur from process cleanup operations and auxiliary facilities. Generally these discharges are similarly low as gaseous discharges. Liquid releases from EURODIF in 1997 were only 9.4×10^{-3} GBq of uranium. Liquid and gaseous releases are summarised in Table 4.

Radioactive discharges from centrifuge enrichment facilities are very small and even lower as from gaseous diffusion facilities. An example is given for the URENCO enrichment plant at Gronau, Germany in the Annex A.

Table 4. **Annual discharges from EURODIF enrichment plant**
(1997 annual throughput: 8 500 tU)

Radionuclide	Gaseous		Liquid	
	kg	GBq	kg	GBq
^{234}U	5.0×10^{-4}	1.2×10^{-1}	2.4×10^{-5}	5.5×10^{-3}
^{235}U	5.6×10^{-2}	4.5×10^{-3}	2.9×10^{-3}	2.0×10^{-4}
^{238}U	3.3	4.1×10^{-2}	0.29	3.8×10^{-3}
Total	3.3	1.6×10^{-1}	0.29	9.4×10^{-3}

UO_2 fuel fabrication

There are a number of PWR fuel fabrication plants in NEA Member countries. The Romans plant of *Franco-Belge de fabrication de combustible* (FBFC) is selected as a reference facility for fuel fabrication in the light of state of the technology, operating period, compatible regulatory requirements to the MOX facility. 650 tHM were processed in 1997 and this is equivalent to a production of 154.5 TWh (17.7 GWa) with a mean burnup of 30 GWd/t.

The Romans plant uses a dry process for UF_6 conversion into UO_2 powder. This process has advantages in reducing liquid and gaseous releases into the environment. Wet conversion processes, however, have also low releases but the amounts of waste generated during effluent treatment are significantly higher.

The UO_2 powder is press-compacted into small cylindrical pellets, then sintered and ground to their final configuration. As a result of this process, the fissile material acquires the physical shape and chemical property suitable for use as nuclear fuel. The pellets are loaded into zircaloy tubes then both ends are sealed (fuel rod). Fuel rods (264 for reference power plant) are positioned within a fuel assembly skeleton and a top nozzle is fitted. After inspection, the complete fuel assembly is ready for shipment to power plants.

For this study, normalised 1997 data per gigawatt-year are used for liquid and gaseous releases. Gaseous and liquid releases from the Romans plant in 1997 are given in Table 5.

Table 5. Discharges from the Romans UO$_2$ fuel fabrication plant (Year 1997)

Radionuclide	Annual activity released (GBq/a)		Annual activity released (GBq/GWa)	
	Gaseous	Liquid	Gaseous	Liquid
^{234}U	1.3×10^{-2}	2.2	7.6×10^{-4}	1.2×10^{-1}
^{235}U	5.2×10^{-4}	8.4×10^{-2}	3.0×10^{-5}	4.8×10^{-3}
^{238}U	2.3×10^{-3}	3.6×10^{-1}	1.3×10^{-4}	2.0×10^{-2}

Radon results indirectly from the natural decay of uranium. The process of uranium ore (U$_3$O$_8$) conversion in several stages to UO$_2$, however, removes all uranium decay products, including radium, the direct parent of radon. Thus, because radium is removed, and because the very long radioactive decay periods of uranium and several of its daughter products that precede radon in the decay chain, there is no radium present in fuel, and thus no radon is emitted. This also applies to the enrichment process.

MOX fuel fabrication

There are three large-scale MOX fuel fabrication plants in operation in NEA Member countries. The MELOX plant is selected as the reference plant. It started operation in 1995 and fabricated 100.3 tHM in 1997, which is equivalent to production of 2.7 GWa with a mean burnup of 30 GWd/t. It will further increase its output to 210 tHM/a by year 2000.

PuO$_2$, depleted UO$_2$ and recyclable scraps in the form of (U-Pu)O$_2$ are blended in order to obtain the required plutonium content. The blended powder is ground and further homogenised, then undergoes the same process as for UO$_2$ fuel fabrication. In the case of the MELOX plant, PuO$_2$ powder is supplied by the reprocessing plant and depleted UO$_2$ powder by uranium enrichment plant, thus liquid and gaseous releases are reduced.

Gaseous and liquid releases from MELOX MOX fabrication plant are lower than the detection level, but it is estimated that they are on the order of 0.01 GBq/GWa.

Generic discharges for conversion, enrichment and fuel fabrication

The generic calculations were undertaken for summed discharges from fuel conversion, enrichment and fabrication. The dominant contribution was from the conversion of UOC to UF$_6$. The assumed annual discharges are given in Table 6. The discharges were normalised to electricity production assuming a reference burnup of 40 GWd/t.

Table 6. Generic discharges from the conversion, enrichment and fuel-fabrication stages
(*Note:* Contributions from enrichment and fuel fabrication stages are negligible)

Radionuclide	Annual discharges (GBq/a)		Normalised annual discharges (GBq/GWa)	
	Gaseous	Liquid	Gaseous	Liquid
^{230}Th	Not discharged	5.2×10^{1}	Not discharged	1.5
^{232}Th	Not discharged	1.1	Not discharged	3.1×10^{-2}
^{234}Th, ^{234}Pa *	Not discharged	1.4×10^{5}	Not discharged	4.1×10^{3}
^{234}U	5.7×10^{-1}	5.5×10^{1}	1.6×10^{-2}	1.6

* Values for thorium and protactinium have been added, based on discharge data for total beta assumed to consist of 50% ^{234}Th and 50% ^{234m}Pa.

3.3 Power Generation

In 1998 some 345 nuclear plants were in operation in NEA Member countries. The most common nuclear power plant in Western Europe is the PWR and this type was assumed in this study. There are a number of plants loaded with MOX fuel and this trend is expected to continue to grow. Radioactive discharges are influenced by site-specific conditions, plant characteristics and national regulatory requirements. The French PWRs have been selected for the study because of the large experience available, including use of MOX fuel. Saint-Laurent 1 is the first in the series loaded with MOX fuel in 1987. Nine French plants were loaded with MOX fuel in 1996 and 17, in 1999. French experience also allows a comparison of radioactive discharges from plants of the same design with and without MOX fuel.

The average content of plutonium in MOX fuel is limited to 5.3%. At equilibrium, the MOX fuel elements represent approximately 30% of the total number of fuel elements in the core.

Typical discharges

A comparison of radioactive discharge data given in the Annex A demonstrates that use of MOX fuel in the reactor did not modify the level of radioactive discharges or their isotopic composition. For this study, normalised 1996 data per gigawatt-year are used on the basis of radioactive discharges/releases data for 900-MWe series. Normalised liquid and gaseous discharges/releases are given in Table 7.

Table 7. **Annual discharges from French PWRs – 1996**
(Normalisation to the unit of electricity produced: 1 GWa)

	900 MWe (GBq/GWa)	1 300 MWe (GBq/GWa)
Liquid discharges:		
• Σ y-emitters*	2.5	1.3
• Tritium	1.47×10^4	1.71×10^4
Gaseous discharges:		
• Gas	$< 7.7 \times 10^3$	
• Halogens and aerosols	$< 7.8 \times 10^{-2}$	

* Sum of the activities of all γ-emitting radionuclides identified.

It should be noted that releases of ^{14}C from French reactors are not measured systematically, but are measured at a limited number of plants. The value adopted for the study is 0.2 TBq/GWa. On average, the atmospheric discharges from German PWRs are estimated at 0.1 TBq/GWa. Releases of ^{14}C in liquid discharges are assumed to represent only a tiny part of the total releases of ^{14}C (approximately 5%).

Reference power generation facility and generic discharges

Annual discharges from a typical 1 300 MW(e) PWR were derived on the basis of French data (Deprés 1999) and are given in Table 8. On the basis of available information, it was assumed that there was no significant difference between discharges from a reactor loaded with UO_2 and one loaded with MOX.

Table 8. **Generic annual discharges from a PWR**

Radionuclide	Annual discharges (GBq/a)		Normalised annual discharges* (GBq/GWa)	
	Gaseous	Liquid	Gaseous	Liquid
^{3}H	9.0×10^2	1.8×10^4	8.4×10^2	1.6×10^4
^{14}C	2.2×10^2	1.6×10^1	2.0×10^2	1.5×10^1
^{41}Ar	3.5×10^1	Not discharged	3.3×10^1	Not discharged
^{54}Mn	Not discharged	1.5×10^{-2}	Not discharged	1.4×10^{-2}
^{58}Co	1.7×10^{-4}	3.7×10^{-1}	1.6×10^{-4}	3.4×10^{-1}
^{60}Co	6.5×10^{-6}	1.7×10^{-1}	6.1×10^{-6}	1.5×10^{-1}
^{63}Ni	Not discharged	$4.0 \; 10^{-1}$	Not discharged	3.7×10^{-1}
^{85}Kr	6.5	Not discharged	6.1	Not discharged
^{88}Kr	2.3×10^{-1}	Not discharged	2.2×10^{-1}	Not discharged
^{110}Ag^m	Not discharged	9.5×10^{-2}	Not discharged	8.9×10^{-2}
^{124}Sb	Not discharged	5.0×10^{-2}	Not discharged	4.7×10^{-2}
^{131}I	1.6×10^{-2}	1.5×10^{-2}	1.5×10^{-2}	1.4×10^{-2}
^{133}I	2.0×10^{-3}	Not discharged	1.9×10^{-3}	Not discharged
^{133}Xe	5.0	Not discharged	4.7	Not discharged
^{134}Cs	Not discharged	6.0×10^{-2}	Not discharged	5.6×10^{-2}
^{137}Cs	Not discharged	1.8×10^{-1}	Not discharged	1.6×10^{-1}

*   An electricity generation of 1.07 GWa was taken in normalising the discharges.

3.4   Interim Storage and Conditioning of Spent Fuel

Storage facilities for spent nuclear fuel assemblies

Irradiated fuel assemblies are stored at reactor sites (AR) or away from reactors (AFR) at reprocessing facilities or separate storage locations. Due to the fact that worldwide no repository for disposal of spent nuclear fuel or high-level radioactive waste is in operation, and only a fraction of spent fuel is going for reprocessing, the main share of spent fuel produced up to now is kept in interim storage. At present, the amount of spent fuel in interim storage is estimated to be 100 000 tHM. Therefore interim storage has to be acknowledged for the time being and the future as an important stage in the nuclear fuel cycle.

Storage in water pools is the common practice for AR storage after unloading the fuel from the reactor core. This practice is part of reactor operation and covered by the corresponding licence. Therefore radiation exposures of plant personnel and discharges have to be within the operation authorisation of the nuclear power station, and are accounted in the corresponding chapter. A similar practice is valid for the large wet storage pools at reprocessing plants and the releases reported cover the whole facility.

AFR spent fuel storage has been implemented in several countries as wet storage in pools or as dry storage using concrete canisters, metal casks or concrete vaults.

Examples for AFR wet storage are the pools for light water reactor (LWR) fuel assemblies in an underground central storage facility CLAB in Sweden and in the store close to Olkiluoto nuclear power plant in Finland. As it became evident that in future large quantities of aged spent fuel with lower heat generation would have to be stored for long time periods, various forms of dry storage have been developed. Roughly three forms of dry storage concepts can be distinguished: metal casks, concrete containers or concrete vaults. An overview of AFR storage capacities and of dry storage concepts and their implementation is given in the Annex A.

Discharges

Discharges from AFR pool storage facilities

Practical experience from the Olkiluoto (Finland) and CLAB (Sweden) AFR storage pools shows that discharges of radioactive substances to the environment are very small. Nuclide-specific discharge data to air and water are available from CLAB for 1996 (see Annex A).

With respect to the comparison of different fuel cycle strategies, the radiological impact of discharges from AFR wet storage facilities on the public is negligible.

Due to the continuous purification of the pool water, spent ion-exchange resins contaminated predominately by ^{60}Co have to be treated for interim storage and disposal.

Discharges from AFR dry storage facilities

No discharges of radioactive substances requiring emission control occur at dry cask storage facilities. During the licensing procedure for the German facilities at Ahaus and Gorleben an assessment has been performed on potential activation of air, dust, moisture and construction material due to the very weak neutron emission from the casks. The results confirmed that no specific precautions are necessary in this respect.

For the dry interim storage facility for VVER (Russian type design of pressurised reactor) fuel assemblies at Paks, Hungary, design basis radioactive discharges have been assessed in the safety case (see Annex A).

In summary, dry storage facilities for spent fuel assemblies show no or only very small discharges of radioactive substances to the environment. For a comparison of fuel cycle strategies this aspect has no relevance.

Conditioning of spent-fuel assemblies for disposal

Irradiated fuel assemblies that are not reprocessed (UO_2 fuel in once-through option and MOX fuel in the reprocessing option) have to be packed or conditioned prior to disposal after the period of wet or dry interim storage. This handling stage has not yet been performed because no repository is operable, and containers for disposal of fuel assemblies in deep geologic formations are still in the stage of development. Different modes of packaging and conditioning have been proposed and are under development. The easiest procedure (proposed to be employed in the probably most advanced national spent fuel disposal plans based; for example; on the Swedish KBS-3 concept) consists just in packaging the complete fuel assemblies in containers suitable for the repository. Other concepts are based on disassembling the fuel bundle to single rods, to rod consolidation or to cutting the rods into few pieces to reduce the length of the container for disposal.

For packaging of intact spent fuel assemblies into containers for disposal, no or only minor radioactive discharges are to be expected. In case of rod consolidation the risk of damage of the rod cladding exists with a potential of the release of volatile radionuclides. For cutting operations ^{85}Kr, ^{3}H and ^{129}I will probably be released together with small amounts of radioactive aerosols.

In the 1987 safety case for the German pilot conditioning plant the discharge data are given as upper limits in the application for a licence (see Annex A). No relevant contribution to this study's comparison is expected from this stage of spent fuel management.

3.5 Reprocessing and Vitrification

There are three PWR fuel-reprocessing plants in operation, La Hague in France, Thorp Sellafield in the United Kingdom, and Tokai-mura in Japan. An older plant, designed to reprocess MAGNOX fuel is located at the Sellafield site. The plant at Tokai-mura is a semi-industrial scale plant. A large plant is under construction at Rokkasho-mura in Japan. For this study, the La Hague plant has the most suitable features: long and stable operating experience, modern technology. Thus, it was selected as the reference reprocessing plant.

The La Hague plant has two main units: UP2, that was brought into operation in 1966 and was refurbished with new technology and reopened with an increased capacity in 1994; and UP3 that started its operation in 1990. A total of 1 670 tHM in the form of spent fuel was reprocessed in 1997 and this is equivalent to 397 TWh (45.3 GWa) of produced electricity, assuming a mean burnup of 30 GWd/tHM.

The spent fuel assembly is mechanically chopped into small pieces and chemically processed to separate uranium, plutonium and waste. Uranium and plutonium are converted in oxide forms. High-level liquid waste is processed and conditioned into stable form. Both buffer storage for spent fuel and interim storage for vitrified products and other wastes are available at the reprocessing facilities. Gaseous and liquid effluents are discharged after treatment and measuring of radioactive contents.

Separated uranium is stored temporarily for future use as feed material for uranium enrichment. Some portion has already been recycled. The separated uranium could be used instead of depleted uranium in the fabrication of MOX fuel. This is not specifically considered for this study.

Reference reprocessing facility and generic discharges

The La Hague 1997 liquid and gaseous discharges (Cogema 1998a, b) have been normalised to 1 GWa to define the generic releases given in Table 9. Normalisation was made with a burnup of 30 GWd/tHM, as suggested by the original data, rather than with the 40 GWd/tHM adopted generally for this study. It is assumed that this should not affect the final results, as a higher burnup would imply more energy extracted from the fuel but also a higher inventory of radioactive nuclides.

The data include the releases from such activities associated with the reprocessing plant as conditioning of uranium and plutonium to oxides, and treatment and conditioning waste, as well as from storage of spent fuel, separated uranium, and waste on the reprocessing site.

Table 9. **Generic discharges from a reprocessing plant**

Radionuclide	Annual activity released (GBq/GWa)	
	Liquid	Gaseous
^{3}H	2.6×10^{5}	1.7×10^{3}
^{14}C	2.1×10^{2}	3.8×10^{2}
^{54}Mn	1.1	
^{57}Co	3.0×10^{-2}	
^{58}Co	3.6×10^{-1}	
^{60}Co	1.1×10^{1}	
^{63}Ni	2.9	
^{65}Zn	3.7×10^{-2}	
^{85}Kr		6.6×10^{6}
^{89}Sr	8.2×10^{-1}	
^{90}Sr/Y	8.2×10^{1}	
^{95}Zr/Nb	8.7×10^{-3}	
^{99}Tc	2.9	
^{106}Ru/Rh	4.3×10^{2}	7.2×10^{-4}
^{125}Sb	3.0×10^{1}	
^{129}I	3.6×10^{1}	3.7×10^{-1}
^{131}I*		2.6×10^{-2}
^{133}I*		6.9×10^{-3}
^{134}Cs	4.6	
^{137}Cs	5.4×10^{1}	1.3×10^{-6}
^{144}Ce/Pr	6.5×10^{-2}	
^{154}Eu	9.0×10^{-2}	
U	1.4×10^{-1}	
^{238}Pu	2.1×10^{-1}	1.7×10^{-7}
$^{239/240}$Pu	1.1×10^{-1}	1.3×10^{-7}
^{241}Pu	4.6	
^{241}Am	1.3×10^{-1}	
^{244}Cm	5.4×10^{-2}	

* These radionuclides come from the spontaneous fission of curium.

3.6 Decommissioning and Dismantling of Nuclear Facilities

Nuclear facilities will eventually be decommissioned and dismantled, and the site may be decontaminated for unrestricted use. As compared to the once-through fuel cycle, the MOX cycle additionally requires fuel fabrication and reprocessing facilities. Radioactive waste generated from the decommissioning and dismantling operation is managed in accordance with national regulatory requirement.

A number of nuclear facilities have been decommissioned and dismantled in NEA Member countries. Experience in decommissioning and dismantling operations shows that radioactive discharges and releases are very small in comparison with the operational phase. In the case of modern plants, greater consideration has been given, at the design stage, to the eventual decommissioning of the plant, and thus even smaller releases are expected from such sites. It has thus been assumed, for the purposes of this study, that the liquid and gaseous discharges from decommissioning activities are negligible.

3.7   Disposal of Solid Waste

Radioactive wastes fall into two broad categories: low- and high- level waste. Low-level waste contains small amounts of radioactive nuclides with short half-lives. Sometimes the low-level waste containing higher amounts of radioactivity or longer-lived radionuclides is referred to as intermediate-level waste. Most waste generated at nuclear facilities is low-level. High-level waste contains large amount of radioactive nuclides with long half-lives. High-level waste includes vitrified waste from reprocessing plant and encapsulated spent fuel (UO_2 or MOX). High-level waste contains more than 99% of radioactivity generated but its volume is very small. Waste generated at MOX fuel fabrication would require similar long-term consideration to this waste due to plutonium contamination.

All waste generated from fuel cycle stages, except mining and milling, is sorted by contamination levels or by nature of waste and conditioned at the site of its generation to facilitate subsequent handling in compliance with the national regulatory requirements. Radioactive waste generated at mining and milling stage is disposed of on the site as described in the mining and milling section.

Low-level and short-lived intermediate-level waste may be disposed of in near-surface repositories or in repositories close to surface. Currently, the option for high-level waste preferred by experts is disposal in deep underground repositories. The objective of solid waste disposal is either to provide complete isolation during the decay period or to provide a possibility to defer the possible releases in the far future and distribute the releases for a long release period.

Discharges/releases

No discharges from repositories for low-level waste and intermediate-level waste are considered in this study. Also for the high-level waste or spent fuel (UO_2 or MOX) the impacts of possible deferred releases are not considered. The reasoning for this is that most probably a complete isolation can be maintained during the time period (500 years) chosen in this study for calculating the collective doses brought about by the different stages of the fuel cycle.

The preferred option for disposal of high-level waste, including spent fuel, is to place it in a deep repository in different types of geological formations. Several programmes to develop such repository are underway in the NEA Member countries. Generic studies have shown that long-term isolation of long-lived radioactive waste is feasible (NEA 2000).

The design for a repository of spent fuel or high-level waste is usually based on a multi-barrier concept applying both natural and engineered safety barriers. The technical barriers usually include the waste form itself, the container for the waste products, and backfilling of disposal holes, tunnels and shafts. The most important natural barrier is the geological host medium, which protects the repository structures and provides effective retaining capacity for most of the radionuclides.

Under the normal evolution of the natural and engineered barriers, assuming no human intrusion, radionuclides contained in the repository have sufficient time to decay to very low levels before any release into the host medium might occur. Any releases would be distributed over a very long period. In particular, radionuclide migration in the various geological media considered for hosting underground repositories is deferred by various physical and chemical retention mechanisms. Consequently, the radioactive inventories and relative radionuclide compositions of the wastes will change during the geosphere migration, however the inventories ultimately reaching the biosphere are not significantly different for the two options. Furthermore, the potential releases into the biosphere would result in concentrations significantly below those due to releases from the other fuel-cycle stages being considered. For this study, it is therefore assumed that any releases from underground repositories need not be considered.

Table 10. **Characteristics of solid waste generation and disposal**

	Once-through option	**Reprocessing option**
Mining and milling	• U-contaminated • low radioactivity but long life • large volume	• Same as once-through option but approximately 20% less
Conversion	• U contaminated • low radioactivity but long life • small volume	• Same as once-through option but approximately 20% less
Enrichment	• U-contaminated • low radioactivity but long life • small volume • (depleted UF_6)	• Same as once-through option but approximately 20% less
Fuel fabrication	• U contaminated • low radioactivity but long life • small volume	• Same as for U contaminated waste but approximately 20% less • Pu-contaminated waste: small volume
Nuclear power plant	• FP and AP-contaminated • LLW and ILW • SF (UO_2)	• Waste: same as once-through • SF: (only MOX) 25% of once-through
Reprocessing	• Not applicable	• Vitrified HLW • Pu-contaminated LLW and ILW: small volume • (separated uranium oxide)
Decommissioning and dismantling	• U, FP and AP-contaminated • mainly low active • large volume	• U, FP and AP-contaminated waste: same as once-through • low-level Pu-contaminated waste: small volume • larger number of facilities to be decommissioned, more waste
Characteristics	• Large volume from mining and milling • SF • single disposal option for SF	• 20% less volume • MOX spent fuel and HLW • Pu-contaminated waste • customised disposal options for long-lived waste (HLW and SF)

AP: Activation product.
FP: Fission product.
HLW: High-level waste.

ILW: Intermediate-level waste.
LLW: Low-level waste.
SF: Spent fuel.

3.8 Transportation

Transportation of radioactive materials is a key activity in the nuclear fuel cycle. Transportation of radioactive materials is regulated by national and international regulations, which are based on the IAEA Regulations for Safe Transport of Radioactive Materials. In the fuel cycle, natural uranium, enriched uranium, plutonium, fresh fuel assembly, spent fuel assembly and conditioned waste are transported.

For transportation considerations, nuclear fuel cycle materials can be divided into two large categories: non-irradiated and irradiated materials. The first category includes mainly uranium ore concentrate (UOC), uranium hexafluoride (UF_6) and uranium dioxide (UO_2), and new fuel, and is common to both options, although the ratio of the volumes involved may differ between them. The second category encompasses spent nuclear fuel removed from the reactors and radioactive waste from the waste conditioning and fuel reprocessing facilities. In the once-through option, all spent fuel is sent for interim storage, and waste-conditioning facilities that are common to both fuel cycles. In the reprocessing option, part of the spent fuel (non-MOX fuel) is sent for reprocessing; from where recovered plutonium is sent to the fuel fabrication plant and high-level vitrified waste to the waste disposal.

All materials to be transported are packed in sealed containers. Non-irradiated material, such as UOC and UO_2 are transported in industrial packages (usually drums), new fuel elements in steel containers. For the chemically more hazardous material, UF_6 steel containers are used. Spent nuclear fuel from PWRs is mainly transported in special casks. Wastes to be transported are mainly packed in drums, placed into containers.

As a consequence of the stringent regulations and the requirements to conduct full scale tests for the containers under severe conditions, these are likely to maintain their integrity and leak-tightness in all anticipated transport situations. Hence no radioactive releases or effluents are expected to arise from transportation activities and the external irradiation of workers and of the public are not significant, as reviewed in Chapter 4.

4. DOSE ESTIMATION FOR WORKERS

For this work, doses to workers have been derived from measured exposures at actual facilities. Figures were taken from information published by operators, national authorities and international organisations, except for disposal of radioactive waste where estimates were made.

It should be noted that in this section, collective doses refer to the sum, for all workers (and in the case of transportation, all exposed members of the public), of all annual effective doses (external plus internal).

The worker doses in this study have been estimated on an annual basis, and have been normalised to the dose due to the production of 1 GWa of electricity. The primary estimate made here has been for the once-through cycle, and it has been assumed that the recycling option uses 20% less uranium than the once-through cycle. Thus, worker doses for the recycling option have been calculated by reducing the once-through doses by 20% in all cases except fuel fabrication and power generation. In these two cases, experience in France and elsewhere has demonstrated that occupational doses do not differ as a result of the use of MOX fuel.

4.1 Uranium Mining and Milling

In Table 11, a summary of occupational gamma and radon progeny exposures for 1997 is shown for two Canadian facilities, Key Lake and Cluff Lake. The annual collective dose for 1997 amounted to 1.8 manSv.

Table 11. **Occupational exposures in Canadian facilities**

Facility	Year	Number of exposed workers	Mean γ dose (mSv)	Maximum γ dose (mSv)	Mean Rn progeny exposure (mSv)	Maximum Rn progeny exposure (mSv)
Key Lake	1997	369	0.40	4.0	0.65	2.1
Cluff Lake	1997	308	2.5	17	2.0	2.6

Note: Mine production was 6 000 t U_3O_8/a for Key Lake and 1964 tU/a for Cluff Lake.

In Table 12, the total exposures for designated workers at the Australian mines, Ranger and Olympic Dam are shown for 1996-97. The collective dose for all Australian mine workers was 1.7 manSv. Data refer to mines only. Olympic Dam data for mill and mine are reported for 1999.

Table 12. Annual occupational exposures for Australian mines and mills (Total exposures)

Facility	Year	Number of workers	Mean total dose (mSv)	Max total dose (mSv)
Olympic Dam mine	1997	421	3.0	9.6
Ranger mine	1997	149	3.8	10.0
Olympic Dam mine	1999	777	2.5	9.2
Olympic Dam mill	1999	504	1.0	4.6

Note: Mine production was 1 740 tUO$_2$ in 1998 for Olympic Dam and 4 178 tU/a for Ranger mine.

Using these figures, and normalising to an electric output of 1 GWa, the estimated annual collective dose for mining and milling is shown in Table 13.

Table 13. Annual collective occupational doses for the mining and milling stages (Year 1997)

Facility	Collective dose (γ) (manSv)	Collective dose (α) (manSv)	Total collective dose (manSv)	Total collective dose (manSv/GWa)*
Key Lake	0.15	0.24	0.39	0.02
Cluff Lake	0.78	0.62	1.4	0.16
Olympic Dam	–	–	1.26	0.18
Ranger	–	–	0.45	0.02

* Normalised to the production and 210 tU/GWa (UNSCEAR 1993).

4.2 Conversion, Enrichment and Fuel Fabrication

UOC to UF$_6$ conversion

For the Comurhex conversion facilities in Malvesi and Pierrelatte, the collective dose in 1997, due to external irradiation, is 0.48 manSv for the 419 monitored workers (those with dose higher than the recording level). The average individual annual dose was 1.1 mSv. Normalised to the produced electricity, an occupational dose of 0.02 manSv/GWa has been reported (EUR 1995). This value has been taken as reference value for the once-through option, the corresponding value for the reprocessing option being 0.016 manSv/GWa.

The range of radiation doses to workers involved in the process operated at BNFL Springfields can be illustrated by information taken from annual dose statistics presented to the site's Nuclear Safety Committee. For the main employee groups involved, in a typical recent year (1996), the mean individual dose was 1.5 mSv. No individual worker received a dose greater than 10 mSv. Collective dose was approximately 0.3 manSv (0.008 manSv/GWa).

Uranium enrichment

Gaseous diffusion process

Occupational doses in gaseous diffusion plants are very small due to the low radioactivity of uranium, and to the fact that the UF$_6$ is hermetically contained during all process steps. Data from

EURODIF show that no annual individual dose above 1.5 mSv occurred in 1997 for more than 1 600 workers, and that the collective dose was 0.019 manSv.

A factor of 1.4×10^{-2} was used in Chapter 6 of the ExternE-Study (EUR 1995) to normalise the occupational collective dose at the EURODIF enrichment plant (0.005 manSv/a normalised to 7×10^{-5} manSv/GWa). The same factor is used in this study to obtain occupational doses of 4×10^{-4} manSv/GWa and 3×10^{-4} manSv/GWa for the once-through and the reprocessing options respectively.

Centrifuge enrichment facilities

Occupational radiation doses in centrifuge enrichment facilities are also very small. Data from Capenhurst and Gronau show that on average the individual doses to workers under radiation monitoring are from 0.2 to less than 0.1 mSv/a. The collective dose at Gronau (nominal capacity 1 800 tSWU/a) in 1994 was less than 0.001 manSv for a real throughput of 760 tSWU (Hörmann 1996). On this basis the following normalised collective doses can be determined: for the once-through option, 2.3×10^{-4} manSv/GWa, for the reprocessing option, 1.9×10^{-4} manSv/GWa.

Fuel fabrication

UO_2 fabrication

Based on the measured individual doses in 1997 and the number of workers at the FBFC Romans Plant, the average annual occupational individual dose is 0.15 mSv/a and the normalised collective dose is 6.6×10^{-3} manSv/GWa.

MOX fabrication

Based on the measured collective dose for the workers (MELOX and subcontractors) in 1997 (1.2 manSv) and the number of workers, the average annual occupational individual dose is 0.53 mSv/a and the normalised collective dose is 0.43 manSv/GWa.

4.3   Power Generation

The exposure of workers is essentially related to the type of reactor, the kind of maintenance, the frequency of fuel reloading operations and the radiation protection practices (EDF 1996, EDF 1997). The NEA evaluated, on the basis of the ISOE database (NEA 1996a), the average collective doses for the period 1994-1996. This showed average collective doses of 1.46 manSv per reactor, 1.43 manSv/GWe installed, and 2.7 manSv/GWa produced (0.31 manSv/TWh), for reactors whose installed power is between 800 and 1 400 MWe. The detailed results appear in Annex A.

The record of accumulated doses from French reactors normalised to energy production is given in Figure 2. In 1996, this normalised dose was 2.7 manSv/GWa for the 900 MWe reactors, 1.0 manSv/GWa for the 1 300 MWe reactors and 1.9 manSv/GWa for all the reactors combined (EDF 1996).

Figure 2. **Trends in the normalised collective occupational dose in French reactors**

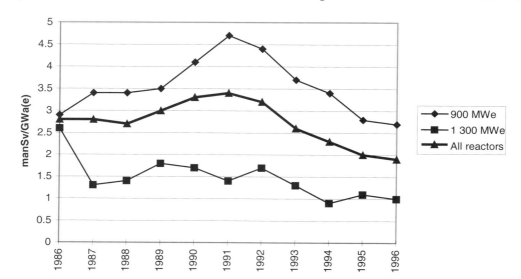

4.4 Interim Storage and Conditioning of Spent Fuel

Pool storage facilities

Because wet and dry away from reactor (AFR) storage facilities in most cases are closely related to other nuclear facilities in the vicinity, as nuclear power plant or waste treatment facilities, occupational radiation doses normally can only be given including service functions of the personnel at these related installations. As an example, most of the occupational dose totalling about 1 manSv/reactor and year at the Olkiluoto NPP is caused by maintenance at the reactor itself during annual outages. Only a very small fraction of the total may be contributed to interim storage operations. For CLAB occupational doses between 1986 and 1996 varied from 0.05 to 0.14 manSv/a depending on the amount of maintenance work performed. Assessing an average of 250 t/a of spent nuclear fuel handled and loaded at CLAB and 25 t/GWa, the occupational doses are approximately 0.005 to 0.014 manSv/GWa.

Dry storage facilities

Present experience with dry storage of spent fuel assemblies is not yet sufficient to derive reliable data on occupational doses. Only very few casks have been transferred to the German AFR facilities at Ahaus and Gorleben. Individual annual doses for the personnel in these facilities are very low. For Ahaus an annual collective dose of 0.0013 manSv has been determined. On the basis of recent studies (Hörmann 1996) an occupational dose of 0.011 manSv/GWa has been assessed for dry cask storage of industrial scale on the basis of annual handling 34 CASTOR-V-19-storage casks holding about 10 tHM each.

Conditioning of spent fuel

Based on the German concept of a pilot conditioning plant with the possibility to perform rod consolidation and rod cutting into about 1 m long pieces in a hot shielded cell a collective dose of 0.026 manSv/GWa has been assessed for a facility of industrial scale.

In the Finnish EIA study (Posiva 1999) for site selection of the encapsulation and disposal facility for spent fuel, the total annual occupational dose for the personnel of the encapsulation and disposal facility is estimated to be 1.24×10^{-1} manSv. Of the total annual occupational dose about 90% is due to the handling operations in the connection of the acceptance of the spent fuel transportation casks to the encapsulation facility. During certain handling operation in this stage it is assumed that the workers are for a short period exposed to the level of 2 mSv/h external dose. The assumed annual throughput of the facility in that case is 184tU of spent boiling water reactor (BWR) fuel corresponding approximately to 5.5 GWa of net electricity production. The normalised occupational dose would then be 2.3×10^{-2} manSv/GWa. It is expected that in practice the occupational dose would be clearly smaller.

4.5 Reprocessing and Vitrification

Table 14 shows the trend in occupational doses at the La Hague plant (Faner and Champion 1999).

Table 14. **Trend in occupational doses at the La Hague reprocessing plant**

Year	Number of monitored workers	Number of exposed workers	Annual collective dose (manSv)	Average annual dose for exposed workers (mSv)	Spent fuel reprocessed tHM	Spent fuel reprocessed GWa	Collective dose (manSv/GWa)*
1988	7 103	2 430	5.85	2.41	346	9.5	0.62
1989	8 210	2 445	4.92	2.01	460	12.6	0.39
1990	8 828	2 307	3.83	1.66	526	14.4	0.27
1991	7 966	1 995	2.97	1.49	662	18.1	0.16
1992	8 525	2 397	2.90	1.21	672	18.4	0.16
1993	9 849	2 250	2.90	1.29	954	26.1	0.11
1994	9 901	1 774	1.92	1.08	1 276	35	0.055
1995	8 778	1 343	1.37	1.02	1 559	42.7	0.032
1996	8 219	1 080	0.91	0.85	1 681	46.0	0.02
1997	7 565	1 009	0.82	0.82	1 670	45.7	0.018

*   A mean burnup of 30 GWd/tHM is used.

The 1997 collective dose received by the La Hague workers, including COGEMA personnel and subcontractors, was 0.82 manSv. The average annual individual dose for an exposed worker was 0.82 mSv. The tasks that contribute the most to the collective dose are mechanical operations (24%) and interventions for decontamination (33%). The normalised collective dose is 0.018 manSv/GWa.

La Hague collective doses have been normalised to the production of 1 GWa of electricity from the reprocessed UO_2 fuel. The reference reprocessing option adopted for this study assumes that about 20% of the energy are produced from plutonium containing fuel (MOX), which is not reprocessed. Consequently, when comparing the two options, collective doses from reprocessing must be scaled down by the ratio of UO_2-fuel amounts entering the PWR in the two options (see Figure 1), namely 21.1 and 26.6 tHM/GWa (ratio 0.79), or by the ratio of mined natural uranium (141.7 and 179.3 tHM/GWa, same ratio).

4.6 Decommissioning and Dismantling of Nuclear Facilities

Much regulatory and industrial attention has been focused on decommissioning activities in recent times, and in many NEA Member countries decommissioning activities are underway at various types of facilities and with various goals. The NEA's International Co-operative Programme for the Exchange of Scientific and Technical Information Concerning Nuclear Installation Decommissioning Projects has, since 1985, worked in this area and has helped to advance the state of the art to that of other comparable industrial-scale activities. Currently, decommissioning activities can be characterised as well understood and fairly standardised (NEA 1996b). Annual collective occupational exposures during decommissioning of all stages of the fuel cycle, including of reprocessing, have been very small, particularly in comparison with worker doses from other stages of the fuel cycle (NEA 1996c, NEA 1999). This is due to the long time period over which decommissioning is conducted, and due to the radiation protection means applied during work activities. Additionally, these doses would be further reduced if normalised with respect to electricity production. For these reasons, these occupational exposures are not further considered in this study.

4.7 Disposal of Solid Waste

In connection with the Finnish EIA study for repository siting estimates were derived for the occupational doses to the personnel of the encapsulation facility (Posiva 1999, conditioning of spent fuel). Based on estimates, it was concluded that the occupational doses are dominated by the encapsulation stage (the acceptance of spent fuel after transportation). Significantly lower exposures (clearly less than 10^{-4} manSv/GWa) would be received by the workers during transfers to the repository, and subsequent emplacement of canisters into disposal holes.

Regarding low-level waste disposal in 1997, doses for ANDRA personnel and subcontractors (representing 629 workers, but only 12 exposed) were the following: the collective dose was 0.0046 manSv and the average annual individual dose was 0.38 mSv for an exposed worker (Faner and Champion 1999).

4.8 Transportation

Concerning the radiological impact from the normal transport operations of radioactive material within the nuclear fuel cycle, mostly fragmentary data are available in the literature. The most comprehensive source of data is constituted by the findings of an IAEA technical committee (IAEA 1986). These results are summarised in the Annex A. Although the data were incomplete in so far as they do not represent a global set and are restricted in some cases to only part of the transportation field in countries, it could be concluded from this report that exposures from normal transport operations are very low both for workers and for members of the public. UNSCEAR, in its 1988 report (UNSCEAR 1988) derived normalised collective dose of 0.2 manSv/GWa and 0.1 manSv/GWa respectively for the occupational and population exposure due to transportation activities within the nuclear fuel cycle from the submissions of the United States and the United Kingdom to the IAEA study. In the UNSCEAR report of 1993 (UNSCEAR 1993) the normalised collective dose value of 0.1 manSv/GWa for the population was confirmed.

Other studies reviewed include:

- French dose estimations to workers and the public on a triennial basis from 1981 to 1990 (Hammard *et al.* 1993);

- a French-German study concerning the return of reprocessing waste material from France (La Hague) to Germany (Gorleben), originating from the German electricity production of 1985-1995 (Fett *et al.* 1997);

- a German study about waste disposal for a once-through cycle, assessing the radiological dose from the transport of spent fuel and low-level waste (Schneider *et al.* 1984);

- results of dose assessments for the normal transport of radioactive materials within the UK up to the year 1989 (Gelder 1992);

- a dose comparison between two nuclear fuel cycles considered for the German situation (Hörmann 1996);

- a comprehensive analysis of health risks brought about by transportation of spent fuel in Finland, where reprocessing is not applied, recently carried out by VTT Energy (Suolanen *et al.*, 1999).

From these studies, normalised collective doses (per unit of nuclear energy produced in the nuclear power plants) have been calculated (see Table 15), taking into account the nuclear energy productions in the corresponding years, in the countries concerned. Because the years during which the transport has taken place may not correspond to the years during which the corresponding electricity has been produced, there may be some uncertainty in the results.

When considering routine transportation of radioactive materials in the three important segments of the nuclear fuel cycle, namely spent fuel, fresh fuel and waste, the differences in normalised collective doses (both occupational and public) between the two options are expected to be quite small; of the order of some 10^{-3} manSv/GWa. The differences may be brought about, on the one hand by the location of the installations, on the other hand by factors that are inherent to the systems. These factors may include the larger amounts of fresh uranium concentrate and spent fuel to be transported in the once-through option, and the larger amounts of LLW and ILW in the reprocessing option.

A recent German study (Hörmann 1996) indicates larger collective doses for the reprocessing option with differences of the order of more than 10^{-2} manSv/GWa for the occupational dose and of an order of magnitude lower for the dose to the public. A Finnish study summarised in (Suolanen *et al.* 1999) also indicates rather high occupational dose values (up to the order of the values for the whole fuel cycle in Germany) for the transport of spent fuel only in a once-through option. As already mentioned the differences in the estimated doses may be explained to a large extent by site-specific conditions (transportation distances, densities of population etc.) and the degree of conservatism in the assumptions of the different studies.

As an overall conclusion the differences in normalised occupational or public exposures from transportation between the two options are small. Furthermore, the contribution of transportation is small relative to the most dominant stages (*i.e.*, mining and milling, reactor operation and/or reprocessing of spent fuel).

The maximum annual individual doses reported range from trivial ones to the public (less than 0.01 or 0.03 mSv) to less than 5 mSv for the workers in Europe.

Table 15. **Normalised annual collective doses for transport**

	Annual collective dose to workers (10⁻³ man Sv/GWa)				Annual collective dose to the public (10⁻³ man Sv/GWa)			
	France	United Kingdom	Germany	Finland	France	United Kingdom	Germany	Finland
Spent fuel	0.2-1.7	1.1-1.6	4.9[1]	5.4–22	Maximum: Half of occupational	0.1-0.3	4.9[1]	1.2-3.3
Non-irradiated fuel	0.1[3]-1.4[2]	0.7			Maximum: Half of occupational			
IL+LL waste	0.2-4.7[4]	1.9			Maximum: Half of occupational	3.3[5]		
Nuclear power plant			25[1]				25[1]	
Conditioning			1.5[1]				1.5[1]	
Reprocessing			2.5				1.2	
HL waste								
Conditioning			0.45[1]				0.45[1]	
Reprocessing			0.12				0.31	
All		36	2.4				2.5	
Once- through			11				1.3	
Reprocessing			28				2.9	

1. Occupational + public dose.
2. Enriched uranium + plutonium.
3. Possibly other radioactive material included.
4. Low-level radioactive waste.
5. Not only waste.

4.9   Summary of Results and Discussion

Detailed doses to workers introduced in the preceding sections are given in Table 16 and summarised in Table 17.

Table 16. Detailed doses to workers at various fuel-cycle facilities

Fuel cycle stage	Facility	Annual collective dose to workers (manSv/GWa)		Average annual individual occupational dose[4] (mSv/a)
		Once-through	Reprocessing (recycle)	
Mining and milling[1]	Key Lake	0.02	0.016	1.05
	Cluff Lake	0.16	0.13	4.5
	Olympic Dam	0.18	0.14	3.0
	Ranger	0.02	0.016	3.8
Conversion[1]	Malvesi and Pierrelatte	0.02	0.016	1.1
	Springfields	0.008	0.006	1.5
Enrichment[1]	EURODIF	0.0004	0.0003	< 1.5
	Gronau	0.00023	0.00019	< 0.2
UO_2 fabrication[1]	Romans	0.0066	0.005	0.15
MOX fabrication	MELOX	–	0.089[3]	0.53
Power generation	French 900 MWe	2.7	2.7*	
	French 1 300 MWe	1.0	1.0*	
	All reactors	1.9	1.9*	
Interim storage	CLAB	0.005–0.014	–	< 0.135
Conditioning	German study	0.026	–	
	Finnish study (EIA)	< 0.023	–	
Reprocessing	La Hague	–	0.014[2]	0.82
HLW disposal	Finnish study (EIA)	< 0.0001	< 0.0001*	
Transportation**		0.005-0.022	0.005-0.028	

*   About the same values as for the once-through option.

**   Normalised doses from transportation are listed in Table 15 by type of waste transported.

1. Collective doses for the reprocessing option have been scaled down by the ratio of mined natural uranium needed for the two options (179.3 t and 141.7 t, ratio 0.79, see Figure 1).
2. Section 4.5).
3. MELOX value (0.43) has been weighted by relative amounts of UO_2 and MOX fuel (21.1 t and 5.5 t, see Figure (1).
4. Average or maximum (<) individual doses.

Table 17. **Dose estimation for workers from major fuel-cycle stages of each option**

Fuel cycle stage	Annual collective dose to workers (manSv/GWa)	
	Once-through	**Reprocessing**
Mining and milling	0.02-0.18	0.016-0.14
Conversion, enrichment	0.008-0.02	0.006-0.016
Fuel fabrication	0.007	0.094
Power generation	1.0-2.7	1.0-2.7
Reprocessing, vitrification	–	0.014
Transportation	0.005-0.02	0.005-0.03
Total	**1.04-2.93**	**1.14-2.99**

The occupational doses involved in the whole fuel cycle are dominated by doses to workers at the nuclear power plant. The occupational doses to workers in nuclear power plant are not affected by the type of fuel used (UO_2 or MOX). At the fuel fabrication stage there is a considerable relative difference between occupational exposures of the two fuel cycle options which is not fully compensated by the differences of collective worker doses at the mining and milling stage. However, the absolute values are only a small fraction of the sum over the whole fuel cycle for both options.

5. METHODOLOGY FOR GENERIC DOSE ASSESSMENT

5.1 Introduction

This report considers the radiological impact on workers and members of the public arising from the various stages of the two fuel cycles options described in Chapter 1. Where possible the report draws upon other studies and upon information published by national and international organisations. However, generic calculations of doses to members of the public from discharges from nuclear fuel cycle facilities were undertaken as part of this study. Results from site-specific assessments were used for comparison.

In calculating doses to members of the public, assumptions must be made about population distribution, habits of individuals and characteristics of the environment in which they live, and about conditions of releases (meteorological conditions, stack height, etc.). These assumptions can have a considerable influence on the magnitude of the calculated doses. For example, following discharges to the marine environment, some radionuclides may transfer to marine life and the magnitude of the resulting dose to an individual will clearly depend upon the amount of the marine foodstuff that he or she consumes. Consumption rates such as these can vary geographically and may also vary with time at the same location. Similarly, the collective dose from, say, discharges to atmosphere will, depending upon the particular radionuclides, be proportional to the population density around the discharging site and also to the agricultural productivity of the surrounding area. This introduces difficulties in making a general comparison of the radiological impact of components of the fuel cycle because the impact of a nuclear fuel cycle facility will depend to some extent on where it is located. Therefore, this study applied a set of standard assumptions in order to compare all stages of the two options on a common basis.

5.2 Radiological Indicators

The principles of radiological protection have been described in Chapter 2. The report uses ICRP recommendations as the basis for assessing radiological impact. The main indicators of the radiological impact are the highest doses to individuals, the "*critical group doses*", and the doses to all the individuals in an exposed population, the "*collective doses*". The former can be compared with dose limits whereas the latter may provide an indication of overall health impact. Long-lived radionuclides, which are released to the environment at some stages in the fuel cycles, may remain in the environment for long time periods causing low-level exposures of members of the public. Following the reasoning presented in Chapter 2, radiological impacts up to around 500 years into the future from releases of long-lived radionuclides are taken into account. Radiological impacts following the disposal of solid wastes from the final stages of the fuel cycles and from decommissioning of fuel cycle facilities are not considered; these materials are, or will be, handled in a controlled manner within the system of radiological protection and, in many cases, materials with similar radiological impacts are likely to arise from both options.

The term "dose" in this report refers to effective dose and is the sum of the annual external effective dose and the committed effective dose from intakes over 1 year integrated to 50 years for adults and to 70 years for infants. Doses were determined in accordance with the most recent recommendations of the ICRP, namely effective dose as defined in ICRP Publication 60 (ICRP 1991) and the dose coefficients presented in ICRP Publication 72 (ICRP 1996). The critical group doses are calculated as individual doses received in the 50th year following continuous discharges at the same level for 50 years. This period was chosen because it is a representative operating lifetime for a facility. Furthermore, the concentrations of most radiologically significant radionuclides will have reached equilibrium in relevant environmental materials (soils, *etc.*) over this time period. Doses via a wide range of exposure pathways were calculated, including ingestion of foods, external exposure and inhalation. The collective doses presented are for a single year's discharge, resulting from the production of 1 GWa of electricity, truncated at 500 years, rather than integrated to infinity.

In order to assist in the comparison of the two fuel cycles, the collective doses to members of the public are normalised to electricity production in GWa. This is not done for the doses to individuals as their magnitude depends upon the particular operating characteristics of the site involved, and thus no distinction between the two fuel cycle options has been made in individual public doses.

5.3   Methodology for Estimating Doses to Members of the Public from Discharges

Generic assessments of doses were undertaken using the models and methods detailed in European Commission Radiation Protection 72 report: Methodology for assessing the radiological consequences of routine releases of radionuclides to the environment (Simmonds *et al.* 1995). This methodology is implemented in PC CREAM 98 (Mayall *et al.* 1997) and BIOS (Martin *et al.* 1991). PC CREAM 98 is a software package for the assessment of routine and continuous discharges of radionuclides to atmosphere, and to marine environments. PC CREAM was developed by the NRPB under contract to the European Commission DGXI. The BIOS code is the NRPB biosphere transport model capable of modelling discharges of radionuclides to rivers and the subsequent calculation of collective doses. Very special ecosystems are not included in these packages.

Discharges to atmosphere

For the calculation of doses from discharge to atmosphere PC CREAM uses a standard gaussian plume dispersion model. A uniform windrose meteorological data file, set up to represent 60% Pasquill category D conditions was used to represent meteorological conditions at all of the sites in this assessment. A single stack of 30 m effective release height was used for all but the mining and milling stages of the assessment. The venting of radon from mill tailings was represented by five stacks set at equal distances to represent an idealised heap of tailings, the central stack having an effective release height of 30 m, whilst the four outer stacks were set to 10 m. The area of the tailings heap was taken to be 100 ha (10^6 m^2), see Figure B1 of Annex B. General assumptions used in calculating doses from releases to atmosphere are given in Table 19.

In all cases the critical group was defined as living at a distance of 1 km from the atmospheric discharge point. With the exception of uranium mining and milling, critical group doses were calculated for the following exposure pathways: inhalation of the plume, external exposure from radionuclides in the plume and deposited on the ground, ingestion of terrestrial foodstuffs, and inhalation of resuspended material. Critical group doses for uranium mining and milling were estimated for inhalation of ^{222}Rn only; it was assumed that the area immediately surrounding the facility was unlikely to support extensive production of terrestrial foodstuffs.

The critical group food intake rates are given in Table 19, and were taken from information supplied by Germany and from reference (Robinson 1996). The intakes of milk and root vegetables were assumed to be taken entirely from a reference production point 1 km from the discharge point, whilst only 50% of the intake of the remaining foods were taken from 1 km. The other 50% of the intake were assumed to be from locations unaffected by the discharge. Adults were assumed to spend 30% of their time outside whilst infants were assumed to spend only 10% (see Table 18).

The assessment of collective doses from atmospheric discharges made use of actual population and agricultural distribution data for Europe for all but the mining and milling stage. The assessment took account of the same exposure pathways as were considered for critical group doses. Where appropriate the contributions from global circulation of radionuclides were included. For the assessment of collective doses from mining and milling a uniform density population grid representing 1 person/km^2 was produced to give results for two separate distance bands, from 0 to 100 km and from 100 to 2 000 km. Such separation will enable the impact of various population density patterns to be assessed. In this way, collective doses were calculated for inhalation of ^{222}Rn. However, it is possible that doses could also be delivered via food chain pathways following deposition of daughter radionuclides of ^{222}Rn onto soils and crops. The significance of this route of population exposure will depend upon the agricultural productivity of the surrounding region. In the absence of detailed information on this, an upper estimate of the collective doses from food chain pathways was obtained by assuming the release occurred from a site in England using European agricultural production data.

Discharges to the marine environment

For discharges directly into the marine environment PC CREAM 98 was used whilst discharges to rivers were modelled using BIOS. These are compartment models where the dispersion of radionuclides is modelled by first order kinetics between defined compartments that represent particular sectors of the environment. The interaction of radionuclides with suspended and river or seabed sediments is modelled. For discharges to the marine environment, doses via the following exposure pathways were calculated: ingestion of fish, crustaceans and molluscs; external exposure from occupancy of beaches; and inhalation of sea spray and of resuspended beach material. In the case of discharges to freshwater systems doses from ingestion of fish and drinking water, and from occupancy of riverbanks were estimated. In estimating critical group doses, all intakes of sea foods were taken from the local marine compartment, which is the model compartment that receives the discharges and where the estimated radionuclide concentrations will be highest; external exposure from occupancy on beaches was also assumed to occur on the beaches bordering the local marine compartment. Except for uranium mining and milling, all freshwater fish and drinking water intakes were taken from the first river compartment downstream of the discharge point. For the uranium mining and milling calculations, the typical concentrations of radionuclides measured in freshwater bodies near uranium mining facilities were taken. Details of the intake rates are provided in Table 19, whilst river bank and beach occupancy rates are given in Table 18. In estimating collective doses, calculated concentrations of radionuclides in environmental materials were combined with estimates of seafood catches and of coastline lengths (see Mayall *et al.* 1997).

Table 18. **Occupancy data**

Occupancy data	Infants	Adults
Distance from discharge point (m)	1 000	1 000
Percentage of time outside (%)	10%	30%
River Bank Occupancy (h/a)	30	500
Beach Occupancy (h/a)	30	2 000
Shielding afforded by habitation (unitless)		
Cloud gamma	0.2	0.2
Deposited gamma	0.1	0.1

Table 19. **Critical group intake data**

Food, drinking water and inhalation rates	Annual consumption rates (kg/a)	
	Infants	Adults
Milk + milk products	200	200
Meat + meat products	10	75
Green vegetables	20	40
Root vegetables	50	60
Cereals	30	110
Fruit + fruit juice	50	60
Freshwater fish	1*	10
Sea fish	5*	100*
Crustaceans	0*	20*
Molluscs	0*	20*
Drinking water	250	440
	Inhalation rate (m^3/a)	
Inhalation rate (m^3/a)	1 900	7 300

*   Taken from (Robinson 1996), remaining data provided by Germany.

6. DOSE ESTIMATION FOR THE PUBLIC

6.1 Introduction

This Chapter describes the doses to members of the public, in terms of critical group doses and collective doses, for each stage of the nuclear fuel cycle. In the generic dose assessment, a set of common standard assumptions for habits, etc., has been used for each stage of the fuel cycle with the exception of mining and milling. The methodology adopted in this approach is given in Chapter 5.

Site-specific calculations, when available, provide an indication of the sensitivity of the results to assumptions about locations and habits, as well as providing further insights into the distributions of doses amongst individuals.

The results are presented in terms of collective doses to the regional population (in all cases except mining and milling, this is the population of Europe) summed up to 500 years. The reasons for summing up to 500 years are given in Chapters 2 and 5. Critical group doses are also estimated in the generic assessment, whereas the site-specific calculations provide information on the collective dose up to 500 years to the local population, which is defined as being within 100 km of the site, and on the dose to average individuals in the surrounding population. The collective doses are normalised to the electricity produced in GWa.

Results are summarised below for each category of facility. Detailed results for the generic calculations are given in Annex B and are summarised in Tables 21 and 22. Doses to the public resulting from transportation are trivial and are consequently not repeated in this chapter. See section 4.8, and Annex A6 for a detailed treatment of the issue.

6.2 Uranium Mining and Milling

Only generic calculations were performed for uranium mining and milling. The main sources of exposure are releases of ^{222}Rn to atmosphere and leaching of ^{226}Ra and daughter radionuclides into local water bodies. ^{222}Rn gives rise to doses by inhalation and also, in some circumstances, to doses from consumption of foodstuffs following the deposition of daughter radionuclides (in this case mainly ^{210}Po and ^{210}Pb). Releases of radionuclides to freshwater systems give rise to doses from the consumption of freshwater fish and from drinking the water.

The critical group for discharges to atmosphere is assumed to reside 1 km away from the mining and milling tailing pile. In the calculations described in Annex B, the heap is assumed to have an area of 100 ha and to release ^{222}Rn at a rate of 3 Bq m^{-2} s^{-1}. The resultant annual dose from inhalation is estimated to be about 0.16 mSv. This dose is proportional to the assumed radon release rate and the area of the tailings; the value chosen for the radon release rate is appropriate for abandoned mill tailings where there is some form of cover reducing radon egress. The exhalation rate for bare tailings can be higher at up to 300 Bq m^{-2} s^{-1}. Some fraction of the tailings would be exposed during the operational phase of the mine but it could be assumed for a well-managed operation that ^{222}Rn exhalation rates averaged over the area of the tailings are unlikely to be more than a factor of two higher than those assumed here. This leads to an estimated critical group dose from ^{222}Rn releases of up to around 0.30 mSv/a.

The majority of large uranium production facilities are situated in areas of very low agricultural productivity and so doses from terrestrial food chain pathways were not considered in assessing critical group doses. However, some radionuclides could be leached from the tailing heap and could contaminate nearby freshwater systems. Therefore, doses via consumption of freshwater and of freshwater fish were evaluated. Typical concentrations of radionuclides measured in freshwater from near to uranium mining facilities were taken. Concentrations of radionuclides in freshwater fish were estimated using standard concentration factors. The estimated dose via these two exposure pathways is, in total, around 0.19 mSv/a for an adult and about 0.25 mSv/a for an infant. In the case of the infant, the majority of the dose arises from the drinking water pathway, whereas for the adult, the consumption of fish is the more important pathway.

It is possible that individuals living near to uranium mining and milling facilities could receive doses via both inhalation of radon and freshwater pathways. Therefore, annual doses to the critical group from uranium mining and milling are likely to be in the range 0.30 mSv-0.50 mSv.

Collective doses from the releases of ^{222}Rn were estimated. Two calculations were undertaken. The first calculation was of the collective dose from inhalation. This is proportional to the number of people exposed. Data on population distributions around uranium mining and milling facilities were not available to this study and so a generic assumption of a population density of 1 person per km^2 out to a distance of 2 000 km was made. Calculations were done for two distance bands, from 0 to 100 KM and from 100 to 2 000 km. The affect of different population densities on the estimate of collective dose can be made by simple scaling.

^{222}Rn by decay produces other radionuclides. Two of these radionuclides (^{210}Po and ^{210}Pb) can give rise to doses via food chain pathways. In order to calculate the contribution from these pathways to the collective dose, data on agricultural production in the affected area is required. These data were not available to this study. Therefore, an upper estimate of the collective dose from food chain pathways was obtained assuming European agricultural production data. In order to undertake this calculation, it also had to be assumed that the uranium mine was located somewhere and for the purpose of the calculation it was arbitrarily assumed to be in the UK.

The collective dose summed up to 500 years to the population within 2 000 km of the mine from inhalation from releases of ^{222}Rn in 1 year is 0.132 manSv; the vast majority of which is delivered to the population within 100 km. Assuming that the tailings from uranium produced for 1 GWa are distributed over 1 ha (UNSCEAR, 1993), this gives a normalised collective dose of 1.32×10^{-3} manSv/GWa. The corresponding estimate for terrestrial food chain production is about 6.7×10^{-2} manSv/GWa. Thus, an upper estimate of the collective dose for releases from a tailings heap over 1 year is about 7×10^{-2} manSv/GWa. Tailings, however, contain very long-lived radionuclides including ^{230}Th (half-life 77 000 years) and ^{226}Ra (half-life 1 600 years), the immediate precursor of ^{222}Rn, and so ^{222}Rn releases could continue for many thousands of years. Nevertheless, the tailings arising from uranium production for 1 GWa will eventually be covered by other tailings and the heap would eventually be capped by an inert layer of material reducing radon emissions. Thus, it is reasonable to assume that the tailings associated with 1 GWa of electricity production would release ^{222}Rn for a period of 10-15 years giving an estimated collective dose of about 1 manSv/GWa. Taking account of the uncertainties in the calculation, the value could lie in the 0.1 manSv/GWa to perhaps a little above 1 manSv/GWa. However, the possibility of protracted releases due to poor maintenance of the tailings cannot be entirely discounted and it is possible that collective doses of tens of manSv could be incurred over 500 years.

The range indicated by results of other studies (UNSCEAR 1993, EUR 1995, SENES 1998) also shows sensitivity to assumptions applied. With similar assumptions the results are largely consistent. More detailed presentation of the results of other studies is given in Chapter A1 of Annex A.

6.3   Conversion, Enrichment and Fuel Fabrication

The generic calculations were undertaken for summed discharges from fuel conversion, enrichment and fabrication. Discharges were assumed to take place at a site in the United Kingdom. The main contribution to the discharges was from the conversion of UOC to UF_6. The estimated doses are very small. Estimated critical group doses from atmospheric discharges were less than 0.001 mSv/a for both adults and infants; the estimates due to discharges to the marine environment were higher at around 0.02 mSv/a for adults and 0.004 mSv/a for infants.

The collective doses per gigawatt-year of electricity to the European population were also very small. Collective doses summed to 500 years to the population of Europe were 6.3×10^{-4} manSv/GWa from discharges to atmosphere and 2.8×10^{-4} manSv/GWa for discharges to the marine environment.

Specific calculations were undertaken for two sites in France. These sites are the UO_2-fuel fabrication plant at Romans and the mixed oxide fuel fabrication plant, MELOX, at Marcoule. The calculated collective doses to the population of Europe summed over 500 years for the Romans plant were 3.0×10^{-4} manSv/GWa for liquid releases and 2.1×10^{-5} manSv/GWa for releases to atmosphere. The corresponding figures for the MELOX facility were 2.5×10^{-3} manSv/GWa and 1.3×10^{-5} manSv/GWa, respectively. These values, although differing by up to around an order of magnitude from the generic calculations, confirm the low overall radiological impact from this phase of the fuel cycle. The detailed calculations show that the majority of the collective dose is delivered to the local population. The average annual doses to individuals in the local population was estimated to be around a few nanosieverts (1 nSv = 10^{-9} Sv) for liquid discharges from both sites with even lower doses from discharges to atmosphere.

6.4   Power Generation

Because the radiological impact depends on the local environment, the generic calculations considered two locations for a typical PWR: one on the Loire River at Dampierre and the other on the north coast of France at Flamanville. The same discharges were assumed for each site.

On the basis of available data it is concluded that there is no difference in discharges between power plants using MOX and UO_2 fuel (see Chapter 3 and Annex A).

For discharges to atmosphere, the critical group doses were similar for both sites at around 5×10^{-4} mSv/a for both adults and infants. For liquid discharges, the critical group dose for adults for the coastal site was around an order of magnitude higher, 3.3×10^{-4} mSv/a, than for the inland site, 4.4×10^{-5} mSv/a. The critical group doses for infants were similar in both cases at around 3×10^{-5} mSv/a. These doses are very small.

Collective doses summed over 500 years to the population of Europe were, in both cases, dominated by the contribution from discharges to atmosphere. For the coastal site, discharges to atmosphere give rise to about 0.53 manSv/GWa; the corresponding figure for the inland site is about 0.63 manSv/GWa. Liquid releases give rise to a collective dose of 0.014 manSv/GWa for the coastal site and 0.02 manSv/GWa for the inland site. The dominant contributor to the total collective dose is ^{14}C.

6.5   Interim Storage and Conditioning

As described in Chapter 3, the discharges from both dry and wet storage facilities, either at reactor sites (AR) or away from reactors (AFR), are negligible. Public exposures from conditioning and interim-torage facilities of the fuel cycles were not considered relevant for this study.

6.6   Reprocessing and Vitrification

The generic calculations indicate that the highest critical group doses are received by adults from discharges to the marine environment. This dose is estimated at around 0.29 mSv/a. About 50% is from the consumption of fish with another 35% from consumption of molluscs. The dominant radionuclide is ^{14}C, which accounts for around 70% of the total dose. Due to the fact that infants are assumed to eat little seafood, the assessed dose to an infant is much lower at about 0.02 mSv/a.

Critical group doses from releases to atmosphere are about 0.11 mSv/a to adults and 0.13 mSv/a to infants. ^{14}C and ^{129}I are the main contributors in both cases. Consumption of grain is the main contributing pathway for adults with consumption of milk being the main one for infants.

Collective doses are dominated by the contribution from atmospheric releases. The collective dose to the population of Europe summed over 500 years from releases to atmosphere is about 1.3 manSv/GWa. Discharges of ^{14}C contribute about 75% with ^{85}Kr contributing about another 17%. The corresponding collective doses from discharges to the marine environment are lower at about 0.234 manSv/GWa; the main contribution again coming from ^{14}C (around 80%).

The generic calculations assume a standard set of habits which may not be applicable to all sites. Calculations using habit data specific to the environment surrounding the La Hague site were also undertaken. Thus estimated, the maximum critical group dose from a combination of discharges to atmosphere and to the marine environment is from 0.005 to 0.059 mSv to inhabitants of nearby villages. The impact of the Sellafield (Thorp) plant, at full throughput, is expected to be no more than a few tens of microsieverts per year to the critical group. Average doses to individuals within 100 km of the La Hague site were estimated at a few nanosieverts from liquid releases and around 5×10^{-4} mSv from releases to atmosphere. Estimated collective doses were similar to those from the generic case and the differences between the two can be explained by the assumptions used, including the fact that the site-specific calculations calculated the collective dose to the population of the European community as it was in 1990, whereas the generic calculations considered Europe as a whole. Discharges to atmosphere contribute about 0.55 manSv/GWa to the population of Europe summed over 500 years, with liquid releases contributing around 0.22 manSv/GWa.

Collective doses from reprocessing have been normalised to the production of 1 GWa of electricity from the reprocessed UO_2 fuel. When comparing the two options, a scaling factor of 0.79 (ratio of UO_2 fuel amounts in the two options) must be applied because about 20% of the energy produced in the reprocessing option come from MOX fuel, which is not reprocessed.

Table 20 provides individual doses to various groups living nearby La Hague. The values are much lower than the value calculated in the generic calculations for the critical group. Several reasons can explain the differences. The distance to the plant is higher than 1 km for all groups considered. The local meteorological data are used to calculate the averaged coefficient of atmospheric transfer. The Doury model of atmospheric transfer corresponds to the French practice. Transfer coefficients in the biosphere may be different and food intakes are substantially lower.

Table 20. **Individual effective dose for specific adult groups living close to the La Hague site (Year 1996, reference: Nord-Cotentin 1999a, b)**

Group	Status of the group	Individual dose (μSv)
Canton de Beaumont-Hague	Average group	5
Digulleville inhabitants	Reference group	6
Goury fishermen	Reference group	5
Huquets fishermen	Critical individuals	26
Pont-Durand farmers	Critical individuals	59
Inhabitants at 1.5 km	Critical individuals	24

Average group: Adults with realistic habits, representative of the nearby county.
Reference group: Adults with realistic habits, identified as the most exposed in the site impact assessment study.
Critical individuals: Adults with extreme habits, considered as possible cases in the dose variability study.

6.7   Disposal of Solid Waste

Radioactive inventories and composition of the wastes of the two options are different. In the case of the once-through option, all radioactive materials in spent fuel are to be disposed of in a deep geological repository. In the case of the reprocessing option, recovered plutonium is recycled, and separated uranium will be temporally stored for future use, either for fuel fabrication or as feed material for re-enrichment. Thus the total quantity of uranium and plutonium to be disposed of is less than in the case of once-through option. However, certain long-lived radionuclides, such as ^{129}I, will ultimately be released to the biosphere, either subsequent to reprocessing or after geosphere migration, regardless of the spent fuel management option chosen. Also, as discussed in Section 3.7, the releases ultimately reaching the biosphere will not differ significantly for the two options, and will be small in comparison to releases from other fuel-cycle stages. Furthermore, one should note the recommendations of the ICRP to consider carefully the use of the collective dose concept in describing the impact of deep repositories during extremely long periods of time. For these reasons, doses resulting from waste disposal are not considered in this study.

Although no release from repository is assumed for this study during the considered time period (500 years), it is worthwhile reviewing progress in safety assessment of deep geological disposal concept, which is a favoured option in the OECD Member counties. A number of safety analyses or performance assessments of deep repositories have been carried out to study the safety and feasibility of disposing either spent fuel or vitrified high-level waste into repositories in different geological media. The level of details in these assessments varies and is dependent on the overall progress of waste management programmes in different countries. The main objective of these studies has neither been the direct comparison of host media nor the different main categories of waste (spent fuel or high-level waste). Rather the intention or objective has been to demonstrate on the one hand the applicability of performance assessment methodologies and on the other hand the feasibility to achieve the required high safety level of waste disposal.

All the results show that it is possible to design the engineered safety features and to locate sites in different host media in such a way that the radiological consequences to hypothetical critical groups in the vicinity of the repositories do not exceed the regulatory constraints. The average doses to larger population groups are much lower.

6.8 Summary of Results and Discussion

The results obtained in the preceding sections are put together for easy comparison in Tables 21 and 22.

Table 21. Dose estimation for the public – Collective dose

Stage of fuel cycle	Pathways	Collective dose up to 500 years (manSv/GWa)		
		Generic calculations		Site-specific assessments
Mining and milling	Inhalation	0.019		
	Food chain [8]	0.981		
	Total (release over 10 to 15 years) [1]	**1.0** (could be up to tens of mansieverts) [2]		1-1 000 (UNSCEAR) [7] 1.6-360 (EC) [7] 0.96 (SENES) [7]
Fuel conversion	Atmosphere	0.0006		0.00002 and 0.00001 [3]
	Liquid	0.0003		0.0003 and 0.0025 [3]
	Total	**Negligible**		
Power production	Coastal, atmosphere	0.53		
	Coastal, liquid	0.014		
	Inland, atmosphere		0.63	
	Inland, liquid		0.02	
	Total [4][5]	**0.54**	**0.65**	
Reprocessing	Atmosphere	1.3		0.55
	Marine environment	0.234		0.22
	Sum [4]	1.5		0.77 (La Hague)
	Total [6]	**1.2**		**0.61**

1. It is assumed that release of a given layer will continue for about 10 to 15 years (see text).
2. In case of poor maintenance of the tailings (see text).
3. Site-specific calculations for Romans and MELOX respectively.
4. Values apply for case where all spent fuel is reprocessed; the dominant contributor is ^{14}C.
5. Mix of coastal and inland sites: 0.6 manSv/GWa.
6. Scaling by the ratio of UO_2 fuel to total amount of fuel (UO_2 and MOX) (see text).
7. See Annex A, Chapter A1.
8. The difference in magnitude between inhalation and food chain collective doses is largely due to the longer integration period for food chain exposure.

Table 22. **Dose estimation for the public – Individual dose (critical group)**

Stage of fuel cycle	Pathways	Average annual individual dose (Critical group) (mSv/a)	
		Generic calculations	**Site-specific assessments**
Mining and milling	Inhalation	0.16-0.30	0.13-0.94 (Canada)[4]
	Fresh water	0.19-0.25[1]	0.02-0.03 (Australia)[4]
	Total	**0.30-0.50**	0.02-0.35 (EC)[4]
Fuel conversion	Atmosphere	$< 10^{-3}$	10^{-6} (Romans and
	Liquid	0.02	MELOX)
	Total	**0.02**	
Power production	Atmosphere	0.0005	
	Coastal site, liquid	0.00033	
	Inland site, liquid	0.00004	
	Total	**0.0005-0.0008**	
Reprocessing	Atmosphere[2]	0.11	
	Liquid[3]	0.29	
	Total	**0.40**	0.005-0.059 (La Hague)

1. For an infant.
2. The dominant radionuclides are ^{14}C and ^{129}I.
3. The dominant radionuclide is ^{14}C.
4. See Annex A, Chapter A1.

Impact on the Public

Generic calculations of impacts on the public have been undertaken by dividing the fuel cycle into four stages: uranium mining and milling, fuel fabrication (including enrichment and uranium conversion), power production, and reprocessing. Results of this study show that the highest radiological impacts come from both the uranium mining and milling stage, and the reprocessing stage. Power production gives rise to collective doses that are similar, for both options, to those from mining and milling and from reprocessing. Critical group doses from power production are, however, very much lower than those from mining and milling or from reprocessing. Fuel fabrication gave rise to the lowest collective doses of any stage.

The assessed collective doses for mining and milling and for reprocessing are similar. This is valid for both the impacts on the general public and on the fuel cycle facility workers. The collective dose summed over 500 years to the regional population (*i.e.,* within a radius of 2 000 km) is up to around 1 manSv/GWa for uranium mining and milling and a maximum of about 1.2 manSv/GWa for reprocessing. Available site-specific calculations support the conclusions of the generic calculations in that the assessed collective dose of an actual reprocessing facility is 0.6 manSv/GWa, and the critical group doses are higher than for the other two stages (*i.e.,* power plant operation and fuel fabrication) of the fuel cycle that were considered.

For both the uranium mining and milling and the reprocessing stages, the generic critical group doses are in the range of 0.30 to 0.50 mSv/a. Actual critical group doses at specific sites can be significantly different, due to differences in the habits and location of local populations, etc. However, the results show that the potential to expose local individuals is similar for these two stages of the fuel cycle.

Based on extensive available data, one can conclude that the introduction of MOX fuel in PWRs has not had any noticeable effect on liquid and gaseous releases from reactors during normal operation. Consequently, the radiological impact of the power production stage is the same for both options.

Uncertainties

The uncertainties associated with public exposure estimates are large. They are associated with the models and scenarios as well as with the underlying parameter values. In particular, uranium mining is very site-specific and doses are strongly influenced by demographics, environmental conditions, characteristics of the uranium containing rock, mining and milling practices, long-term stability of disposed tailings, as well as procedures for maintenance and remedial actions. Actual ^{222}Rn emanation rates could be significantly different from those assumed in this study, leading to higher or lower collective doses. Indeed, if the tailing piles were partially uncovered following a period of poor maintenance, collective doses of up to a few tens of mansieverts par gigawatt-year would be possible.

Limitation at 500 years

Collective doses to members of the public require a critical examination. Collective doses have been summed up to 500 years into the future. It would be possible to sum these doses for longer time periods, including infinity. As collective doses from major stages of the fuel cycles (mining and milling, power production and reprocessing) involve long-lived radionuclides, such an approach would lead to larger collective doses per gigawatt-year of electricity. However, this is unlikely to affect the conclusions of the study for the following reasons. The majority of the collective dose summed over 500 years for both power production and reprocessing arises from the relatively long-lived, mobile radionuclide ^{14}C (half-life 5 730 years). Thus extension of the time period considered is not likely to alter the ratio of the impacts of these two processes. For the mining and milling stage, the production of ^{222}Rn in tailings will continue at a slowly declining rate for a period of hundreds of thousands of years because it is supported by the very long-lived radionuclide ^{230}Th (half-life 77 000 years). While the contribution to the collective doses from this part of the fuel cycle could be considerable if summed over very long time periods, and could even become the dominant fraction, the ratio of collective doses from the two options will not change significantly. For these reasons, and because of the large uncertainties associated with scenarios in the far future, longer summation periods have not been considered in the study.

Mining and milling reduction *versus* reprocessing

The mining and milling, power production and reprocessing stages dominate the collective doses to the public. While power production causes the same radiological impacts for both fuel cycle options, the variations in the radiological impacts of the other two stages tend to be in opposite directions. By reprocessing and through the use of MOX fuel, the need for natural uranium could be reduced by about 21%, and consequently the public and worker exposures caused by the mining and milling stage should be reduced in the same proportion. On the other hand, the reprocessing stage adds to the public and worker collective doses as compared to the once through cycle. However, it should not be forgotten that the assessed public collective doses, and the overall radiological comparison of options, are highly sensitive to assumptions regarding good mill-tailing pile management.

Important nuclides

Only a few radionuclides are important. The main contributor to the total collective dose for power production is ^{14}C. For reprocessing, ^{14}C again, with ^{129}I and ^{85}Kr, dominates radiological impacts. These radionuclides, which are discharged at levels in compliance with regulations, disperse in the environment but are at levels that can still be measured with modern technology. They constitute a potential source of very low doses to the population on a global scale.

The main sources of exposure from the uranium mining and milling stage are daughter nuclides of the naturally occurring uranium decay chains. These represent another potential source in the long-term and on a regional scale.

Disposal of solid waste

In the very long term, radionuclides from an underground repository for HLW or spent fuel could also become a potential source of exposure. Model calculations show that only after several hundreds of thousands of years, a small radiological impact occurs, which is related to ^{129}I, ^{135}Cs, or ^{99}Tc depending on the characteristics of the repository. Collective doses are composed of very small individual doses to a large number of people over a long period of time. Because these doses are small and are expected to be similar for both fuel cycles considered in the study, they have not been included in the comparative analysis.

7. CONCLUSIONS

The general conclusions of the study are provided in this chapter, together with a summary table of main results and references to sections where more details are presented. An overview of the objectives, scope, results and conclusions can be found in the Executive Summary provided at the beginning of this report, however it should be recalled that the use of current practices and current technology has been assumed, and tailings from mining and milling are assumed to be stable in the long term.

Table 23. Summary table of dose estimation for the public and workers
from major fuel cycle stages of each option
(*Note:* Collective doses in this report are used only in a comparative fashion)

Fuel cycle stage	Public (generic calculations)		Average annual individual dose to the critical group (mSv/a)	Workers (operational data)	
	Collective dose truncated at 500 years (manSv/GWa)			Annual collective dose (manSv/GWa)	
	Once-through	Reprocessing		Once-through	Reprocessing
Mining and milling	$1.0^{(5)}$ $(1\text{-}1\ 000)^{(3)(4)}$	$0.8^{(1)\,(5)}$ $[0.8 \times 1\text{-}1\ 000)]^{(3)(4)}$	0.30-0.50 $(0.020\text{-}0.940)^{(3)}$	0.02-0.18	$0.016\text{-}0.14^{(1)}$
Fuel conversion and enrichment	0.0009		$0.020\ (10^{-6})^{(3)}$	0.008-0.02	$0.006\text{-}0.016^{(1)}$
Fuel fabrication				0.007	$0.094^{(2)}$
Power generation	0.6	0.6	0.0005-0.0008	1.0-2.7	1.0-2.7
Reprocessing, vitrification	Not applicable	$1.2^{(1)}\ (0.6)^{(3)}$	0.40 $(0.005\text{-}0.059)^{(3)}$	Not applicable	$0.014^{(1)}$
Transportation	Trivial	Trivial	Trivial	0.005-0.02	0.005-0.03
Disposal	(6)	(6)	(6)	Trivial	Trivial
Total	**1.6**(5)	**2.6**(5)	**Not applicable**	**1.04-2.93**	**1.14-2.99**

1. Collective doses for the reprocessing option have been scaled down by the ratio of mined natural uranium needed for the two options (179.3 t and 141.7 t, see Figure 1).
2. Weighted by UO_2 and MOX-fuel amounts (21.1 t and 5.5 t, see Figure 1).
3. Site-specific assessment values are given within brackets. They provide an indication of the sensitivity of results to assumptions about population distribution, habits of individuals and characteristics of the environment in which they live, and about conditions of releases.
4. The range refers to the sensitivity discussed in other studies UNSCEAR, SENES, EC, using longer integration times (see Table 21 and Annex A1).
5. Collective doses from mining and milling could be a few tens of manSv in case of poor tailing-pile maintenance.
6. As explained in Chapter 6, no releases of radionuclides are expected within the first 500 years after placement of waste and spent fuel in a final repository.

The uncertainties associated with public-exposure estimates are large. They are associated with the models and scenarios as well as with the underlying parameter values. In particular, uranium mining is very site-specific and doses are strongly influenced by demographics; environmental conditions, characteristics of the uranium-bearing rock, mining and milling practices, long-term stability of disposed tailings, as well as procedures for maintenance and remedial actions. Actual ^{222}Rn emanation rates could be significantly different from those assumed in this study, leading to higher or lower collective doses. Indeed, if the tailing piles were partially uncovered following a period of poor maintenance, collective doses of up to a few tens of mansieverts per gigawatt-year would be possible.

Impacts on workers

Doses to workers are estimated in Chapter 4. Collective doses normalised to electricity production from major fuel cycle stages of each option are summarised in Table 23.

Figures are briefly analysed in Section 4.9. There is no significant difference between both options. The impact on workers is dominated by the contribution at the power-generation stage. The occupational doses to workers in nuclear power plants are not affected by the type of fuel used (UO$_2$ or MOX).

Impacts on the public

In calculating doses to members of the public, assumptions have to be made about population distribution, habits of individuals and characteristics of the environment in which they live, and about conditions of releases (meteorological conditions, stack height, etc.). These assumptions influence the magnitude of calculated doses, which introduces difficulties in making a general comparison of radiological impacts of stages of the fuel cycle because the impact of a particular nuclear fuel cycle facility will depend to some extent on where this facility is located. Therefore, the report embodies a set of standard assumptions and generic models as a basis for comparing all stages of the two fuel cycles on a common basis. This procedure is referred to as "generic calculation". "Site-specific calculations", when available, provide an indication of the sensitivity of the results to these assumptions, as well as further insights into the distributions of doses amongst individuals.

The methodology for estimating doses to members of the public from discharges is described in Chapter 5. Technical information on the generic calculations, including tables of doses broken down by radionuclide and pathway, can be found in Annex B. Detailed results for major fuel cycle stages are presented in Chapter 6. Individual doses to critical groups, as well as collective doses calculated over 500 years are summarised in Table 23 together with results from site-specific studies, when available.

A detailed analysis of these figures is provided in Section 6.8. The most important result of the study is that total radiological impacts (collective dose per unit of electricity produced) on the general public from the two fuel cycle options are very similar taking into account the uncertainties involved. It is emphasised that collective doses in this report are used only in a comparative fashion.

The differences between the two fuel cycles examined in the report are small from the standpoint of radiological impact. In this connection, it is simply not justifiable to draw definitive conclusions from the small differences in collective and individual radiological impacts; especially taking into account limitations inherent in the generic calculations. Consequently, radiological impact is not a key factor favouring one option or the other. Rather, other factors such as resource utilisation efficiency, energy security, and economics would tend to carry more weight in the decision-making process. Overall, the public exposures in both options are low compared to the pertinent regulatory limits, and also insignificantly low compared with exposures from natural background radiation (the world wide average annual individual dose from natural radiation is 2.4 mSv).

Trends, progress and open issues

Discharges from all stages of the nuclear fuel cycle have been diminishing in recent years on the basis of feedback from operating experience and the application of new technology and improved procedures. This is in particular true for releases from reprocessing plants.

It is probably possible to further reduce releases from reprocessing facilities. Moreover, adequate remedial actions exist to reduce to insignificant levels long-term radiological impacts caused by radon exhalation from mining and milling tailing piles, but it seems difficult to reduce further the radon release during the operating phase of mining and milling. However, it is important to note that long-term radiological impacts could increase considerably if the remedial actions for tailings are not handled properly.

Behaviour of radioactive substances in the environment has been studied extensively; which has resulted in improvement of models for assessing radiological impacts. Furthermore, research on radiological impacts on living organisms is in progress, but further efforts are needed to confirm the validity of the present approaches by the international organisations described in Chapter 2.4.

Regulatory authorities are carrying out detailed safety studies before authorising discharges. Uncertainties with respect to scenarios and models are taken into account, often by applying conservative hypotheses. It is important to note that discharges considered in this study are much below present regulatory limits.

Doses to workers of nuclear installations have been reduced in recent years. Efforts in that direction will continue even if the level of doses has been well below regulatory limits.

The release of ^{14}C is the dominant source of very low doses to the population on a regional and global scale for both options. The issues surrounding these releases should be further studied from radiation protection, technology, resource implication and societal points of view, even though its contribution is low in comparison with natural radiation.

Depleted and separated uranium are stored at the enrichment-plant and reprocessing-plant sites, respectively, for future use. In some Member countries, it is considered that depleted uranium should be converted into a stable form for eventual disposal. Some proportion of separated uranium is used as feed material for enrichment.

Various disposal options are available for management of low- and intermediate-level waste. Disposal of long-lived waste in deep geological formations is in development as the preferred option among experts in Member countries.

Need for further studies

For the purpose of this report, assumptions have been made regarding the use of collective dose to compare radiological impacts, the management of depleted and separated uranium, the management of MOX fuel, the long-term safety assessment of geological disposal, etc. This methodology may need to be re-evaluated in the future in light of developments such as new environmental transfer models, changes affecting the system of radiation protection (including the use of collective dose), new impact indicators for the environment, etc.

A comprehensive comparison of the two spent fuel management options would necessarily involve a broad range of other issues in addition to radiological impact raised by the normal operation of fuel cycle facilities. These issues would include environmental protection, waste management, resource utilisation efficiency, energy security and economics. In the plant-specific regulatory process, the consideration of incidents and other abnormal events is required. These other aspects are not addressed in this report since they are outside its scope. It is anticipated, however, that this report will serve as a basis for broader studies on nuclear power development strategy, nuclear fuel cycle strategy and nuclear development in the context of sustainable development.

MEMBERS OF THE EXPERT GROUP

Mr. Tomohiro ASANO
Japan Nuclear Cycle Development Institute
Tokyo, Japan

Mr. Jean BRENOT
IPSN, Commissariat à l'énergie atomique
Fontenay-aux-Roses, France

Mr. Gábor BUDAY
Public Agency for Radioactive Waste Management
Paks, Hungary

Mr. John COOPER
National Radiological Protection Board
Chilton, Didcot, United Kingdom

Mr. Christian DEVILLERS
IPSN, Commissariat à l'énergie atomique
Fontenay-aux-Roses, France

Mr. David H. DODD
NRG
Petten, The Netherlands

Mr. Jean-François LECOMTE
IPSN, Commissariat à l'énergie atomique
Fontenay-aux-Roses, France

Mr. Mark LOOS
SCK/CEN
Mol, Belgium

Mr. Chong Mook PARK
KEPCO
Taejon, Korea

Mr. David POLLARD
Radiological Protection Institute of Ireland
Dublin, Ireland

Mr. Hermann PUCHTA
Mr. Ian HALL
CEC DG XI/C/1
Luxembourg

Ms. Synnöve SUNDELL-BERGMAN
Swedish Radiation Protection Institute (SSI)
Stockholm, Sweden

Mr. Wolfgang THOMAS
Gesellschaft für Anlagen- und
Reaktorsicherheit (GRS)
Garching, Germany

Mr. Armando URIARTE
ENRESA
Madrid, Spain

Mrs. Michèle VIALA
IPSN, Commissariat à l'énergie atomique
Fontenay-aux-Roses, France

Mr. Seppo VUORI (*Chairman*)
VTT Energy
Espoo, Finland

Mr. Clive WILLIAMS
Environment Agency
Bristol, United Kingdom

Mr. Theo ZEEVAERT
SCK/CEN
Mol, Belgium

CONSULTANTS TO THE EXPERT GROUP

Mr. A. CIGNA (Consultant)
Cocconato, Italy

Mr. E. HÖRMANN (Consultant)
Gesellschaft für Anlagen und
Reaktorsicherheit (GRS)
Cologne, Germany

NEA SECRETARIAT

Mr. Ted LAZO
OECD Nuclear Energy Agency
Issy-les-Moulineaux, France

Mr. Hans RIOTTE
OECD Nuclear Energy Agency
Issy-les-Moulineaux, France

Mr. Bertrand RÜEGGER (*Secretary*)
OECD Nuclear Energy Agency
Issy-les-Moulineaux, France

Mr. Makoto TAKAHASHI
OECD Nuclear Energy Agency
Issy-les-Moulineaux, France

BIBLIOGRAPHY

COGEMA (1998a), « Rejets liquides en mer effectués par l'établissement de La Hague, année 1997 », HAG/0/5500/98/00030/00.

COGEMA (1998b), « Rejets gazeux de l'établissement de La Hague, Année 1997 », HAG/0/5500/98/00055/00.

DEPRÉS, A. (1999), Personal communication (Releases from PWR).

EDF (1996), « Électricité de France – Production transport, Département Sécurité Radioprotection Environnement, Résultats Sécurité Radioprotection Incendie 1996 ».

EDF (1997), « Électricité de France – Production transport, Département Sécurité Radioprotection Environnement », Activity Report 1997 – Environment Appendix.

EUR (1995), *ExternE Externalities of Energy, Vol. 5: Nuclear*. European Commission Report EUR 16524 EN.

FANER, N. et CHAMPION, M. (1998), « Bilan des expositions professionnelles aux rayonnements ionisants en France sur la période 1990-1997 », IPSN, Rapport SAER n° 43, 1999.

FETT, H.-J., LANGE, F. *et al.,* "Transport risk assessment study for reprocessing waste materials to be returned from France to Germany. IPSN, CEPN, GRS Final Report", GRS 141, Gesellschaft für Anlagen- und Reaktorsicherheit (GRS) mbH, Cologne, 1997.

GARNIER-LAPLACE, J., *et al.* (1993), « Suivi radioécologique des centrales nucléaires françaises (Spectrométrie γ) Année 1992 », Institut de protection et de sûreté nucléaire, Document SERE/94/030 (P), septembre 1993.

GELDER, R., "Radiation Exposure from the normal transport of radioactive materials with the United Kingdom. 1991 Review", NRPB-R255, National Radiological Protection Board, Chilton, Didcot, 1992.

HAMMARD, J., RINGOT, C. *et al.,* "Estimation of the individual and collective doses received by workers and the public during the transport of radioactive materials in France between 1981 and 1990", Proceedings 10th International Symposium on the Packaging and Transport of Radioactive Materials (PATRAM), Vol. 1, p.67-73, Yokohama, 1993.

HÖRMANN, E. (1996), "Aktualisierung des Sicherheitsvergleichs zwischen Wiederaufarbeitung und Direkter Endlagerung sowie des Kenntnisstandes zur Konditionierung abgebrannter Brenn-elemente", Unterauftrag zu BMU-Vorhaben SR 2986, August 1996.

IAEA (1980), *International Nuclear Fuel Cycle Evaluation* (INFCE).

IAEA (1986), "Assessment of the radiological impact of the transport of radioactive materials", IAEA-TECDOC-398, IAEA, Vienna.

IAEA (1999), "Protection of the Environment from Ionising Radiation", IAEA-TECDOC-1091.

ICRP (1977), "Recommendations of the International Commission on Radiological Protection", ICRP Publication 26, Pergamon Press, Oxford.

ICRP (1991), "1990 Recommendations of the International Commission on Radiological Protection", ICRP Publication 60, Annals of the ICRP, 21, Nos. 1-3, Pergamon Press, Oxford.

ICRP (1996), "Age-dependent doses to members of the public from intakes of radionuclides: Part 5 compilation of ingestion and inhalation dose coefficients", ICRP Publication No. 72, Annals of the ICRP, Vol. 26, No. 1.

ICRP (1998), "Radiological Protection Policy for the Disposal of Radioactive Waste", ICRP Publication No. 77, Annals of the ICRP, Vol. 27 Supplement, Pergamon Press, Oxford.

MAYALL, A. *et al.* (1997), *PC CREAM User guide*. NRPB-SR296, EUR 17791.

MARTIN, J.S., BARRACLOUGH, I.M. *et al.* (1991), *User guide for BIOS_3A*. Chilton, NRPB-M285.

MERLE-SZEREMETA, A. (1998), Calculs préliminaires effectués dans le cadre du GT3 du Groupe Radioécologie Nord-Cotentin, Memorandum SEGR/SAER/98-42 (July 1998).

NEA (1996a), "OECD Nuclear Energy Agency – International Atomic Energy Agency, Occupational Exposures at Nuclear Power Plants, Sixth Annual Report (1986-1996)".

NEA (1996b), "The NEA Co-operative Programme on Decommissioning: the First Ten Years".

NEA (1996c), *EUROCHEMIC: European Company for the Chemical Processing of Irradiated Fuels (1956-1990)*.

NEA (1999), OECD Nuclear Energy Agency – International Atomic Energy Agency, Occupational Exposures at Nuclear Power Plants, Eighth Annual Report (1998).

NEA (2000), *Geological Disposal of Radioactive Waste: Review of Developments in the Last Decade*.

NORD-COTENTIN (1999a), « Rapport du GT4, Groupe Radioécologie Nord-Cotentin », juillet 1999.

NORD-COTENTIN (1999b), « Groupe Radioécologie Nord-Cotentin, Rapport final, Tome 4 », juillet 1999.

PENTREATH, R.J. (1998), "Radiological Protection Criteria for the National Environment"; in *Rad. Prot. Dosim.*, Vol. 75 (1-4), p.175-179.

PENTREATH, R.J. (1999), "A system for radiological protection of the environment: some initial thoughts and ideas", *J. Radiol. Prot.* Vol. 19, 117-128.

POSIVA (1999), "The final disposal facility of spent nuclear fuel – Environmental impact assessment report, Main Report", Posiva Oy, Helsinki, 1999.

ROBINSON, C.A. (1996), "Generalised habit data for radiological assessments", NRPB-M636, Chilton.

SCHNEIDER, K., JOBST, C., BERGMAN, W.and HILBERT, F., "Technisches Konzept und Sicherheitsanalyse des Transports von Endlagergebinden mit abgebrannten Brennelementen", Anschlussbericht, Technischer Anhang 5, KWA 3302/0, KWA 3310/7 in "Andere Entsorgungstechniken. F+E Schwerpunkt des Bundesministerium für Forschung und Technologie", Transnuklear GmbH, NUKEM GmbH, Hanau, 1984.

SENES (1998), "Long-term population dose due to radon (Rn-222) released from uranium mill tailings", SENES Consultants Limited.

SIMMONDS, J.R., LAWSON, G. and MAYALL, A. (1995), "Methodology for assessing the radiological consequences of routine releases of radionuclides to the environment", Luxembourg, EC, EUR 15760.

STORCK, R. and BUHMANN, D. (1998), "A comparison of long-term safety aspects – concepts for disposal of spent fuel and wastes from reprocessing", in *Nuclear Technology*, Vol. 121, February 1998, p. 212 –220.

SUOLANEN, V., VUORI, S., and PÖLLÄNEN, L., "Risk analysis of spent fuel transportation related to EIA for repository site evaluation", Nuclear Europe Worldscan. (1999), Nos. 5-6, pp. 42-43.

UNSCEAR (1988), United Nations Scientific Committee on the Effects of Atomic Radiation (UNSCEAR): "Sources, Effects and Risks of Ionizing Radiation, 1988, Report to the General Assembly, with annexes", United Nations, New York, 1988.

UNSCEAR (1993), United Nations Scientific Committee on the Effects of Atomic Radiation (UNSCEAR): "Sources and Effects of Ionizing Radiation, 1993, Report to the General Assembly, with annexes", United Nations, New York, 1993.

UNSCEAR (1996), "Effects of radiation on the environment". In *Sources and Effects of Ionizing Radiation*, 8-86, United Nations Scientific Committee on the Effects of Atomic Radiation UNSCEAR 1996, Report to the General Assembly, with Scientific Annex, United Nations, New York.

WOODHEAD, D. (1998), *The Impact of Radioactive Discharges on Native British Wildlife and the Implications for Environmental Protection*. Environment Agency R&D Technical Report P135, Environment Agency, Bristol, United Kingdom.

Annex A

TECHNICAL SITE-SPECIFIC INFORMATION

Table of contents

A1. Uranium Mining and Milling 71
    Reference sites 71
    Site-specific dose assessments 72
    Bibliography 74
A2. Conversion, Enrichment and Fuel Fabrication 75
    Reference sites 75
    Bibliography 77
A3. Power Generation 78
    Discharges from French PWRs 78
    Doses to workers in some NEA Member countries 81
    Bibliography 82
A4. Reprocessing and Vitrification 83
    Trends over time of discharges of the la Hague 1997 reprocessing plant 83
    Bibliography 83
A5. Interim Storage and Conditioning of Spent Fuel 84
    Reference sites 84
    Bibliography 85
A6. Transportation 86
    Reference data 86
    Bibliography 88

List of figures

Figure A1. Annual liquid discharges from French 900 MWe PWR 78
Figure A2. Annual liquid discharges from French 1 300 MWe PWR 79

List of tables

Table A1. Discharges of radionuclides in liquid effluent from BNFL Springfields, 1995-1997 75
Table A2. Discharges of radionuclides from conversion facilities of Malvesi/Pierrelatte 75
Table A3. Discharges from GRONAU enrichment plant (1 800 tSWU/a) 76
Table A4. Gaseous releases from MELOX MOX fuel fabrication plant, 1997 76
Table A5. Liquid releases from MELOX MOX fuel fabrication plant, 1997 76
Table A6. Occupational doses at EURODIF in 1997 77
Table A7. Isotopic composition of liquid discharges from two French reactors in 1996 79
Table A8. Isotopic composition of the discharge gases from two French reactors in 1996 80
Table A9. Change in liquid discharges from two French 900 MWe
           and 1 300 MWe-type reactors 80

Table A10.   Change in gaseous discharges from two French 900 MWe and
             1 300 MWe-type reactors   81
Table A11.   Normalised annual collective dose to workers (mean 1994-1996)   81
Table A12.   Discharges from CLAB in 1996   84
Table A13.   Design basis radioactive discharges for Paks interim spent fuel storage facility
             according to the safety case   85
Table A14.   Pilot conditioning facility Gorleben: Proposed maximum discharges in the safety case   85
Table A15.   Radiological impact from transport in the nuclear fuel cycle.....................................   89
Table A16.   Radiological impact from transport in the nuclear fuel cycle   90
Table A17   Normalised collective doses from transport in the nuclear fuel cycle   91

70

A1. URANIUM MINING AND MILLING

Reference sites

Data for Key Lake and Cluff Lake presented in this section were obtained from the Atomic Energy Control Board, Canada. Data for Olympic Dam and Ranger mine were obtained from Supervising Scientist Group, Australia and Copper Uranium Division, WMC.

Key Lake, Canada

The Key Lake operation located in the south-eastern portion of the Athabasca basin of northern Saskatchewan in Canada includes open-pit mining of two ore-bodies (Gaertner and Deilmann) were exhausted in 1998. Key Lake has produced approximately 6000 tU_3O_8/a (average grade of 2%) since 1986.

A neighbouring orebody, McArthur River, is located about 70 km north-east of Key Lake. The geological reserve of the site is estimated to contain about 91 000 t at an average grade of 4% U_3O_8. Ore from both the Key Lake (98/99) and the McArthur River has been and will be milled at the Key Lake milling facility. Production is planned to remain relatively constant for the next few years fom the milling of Key Lake ore reserves and McArthur River ore.

The above ground tailings storage facility will store all tailings produced from the milling of the Gaertner and Deilmann deposits using a subgaseous technique. The final design volume of the tailing milling facility is approximately 5.8×10^8 m^3.

There are approximately 80×10^6 t of waste rock (< 4 000 tU_3O_8) at Key Lake defined as less than 0.05% of U_3O_8. Upon decommissioning, the waste rock will be disposed of within the mined-out open-pits or disposed of at another approved waste impoundment site.

There are indications that the content of As and nickel in the waste rock is of more concern than the radioactivity in view of potential environmental impacts. The economical feasibility of extracting Ni and Co from the tailings is therefore being examined.

The population density around the Key Lake area is low. In the SENES report (SENES 1998), the densities were estimated to be 0.034 and 0.63 person/km^2 in the < 100 km and 100-2 000 km regions respectively, based on Canadian and U.S. demographic data.

Cluff Lake, Canada

The Cluff Lake Project, consisting of two operational underground mines, four mined out open-pits, one mill and a tailings management area, is located in Northern Saskatchewan. In 1997, the uranium production balance for the mill was 1 964 tU. The average grade of uranium is 0.6%. Some of the uranium deposits found also contain economic concentrations of gold.

The tailings containment is a valley fill site with seepage control by means of bentonite /till cut-off. After decommissioning it is planned to consolidate limes in a stable form within the tailings and stabilise in place by covering with local material to approximately 1 m thick. The original capacity design of the tailing area is about $2 \times 10^6 \, m^3$.

The population densities around the mining site are similar to the Key Lake site (SENES 1998).

Olympic Dam, Australia

Olympic Dam is an underground copper/gold/silver/uranium mine located 560 km north of Adelaide. The nearest town is Roxby Downs, located some 16 km south of the Olympic Dam operations. The ore body is up to some 5 km long and up to 2.5 km wide. Total resources are 1 650 million t of ore, of average grade 1.1% Cu, 0.4kg/tU and 0.5 g/tAu (WMC Limited Annual Report 1998). The production in 1998 was 1 740 tUO$_2$.

The tailings are currently deposited in two ring-dyke armoured clay lined structures comprising one of three cells totalling 190 ha and 13 m high, and another commissioned in April 1999 of area 190 ha and 7.5 m high (Olympic Dam Corporation Environmental Management and Monitoring Report, 1999). Upon decommissioning it is intended to cap the tailings storage facility with a 1-m radon barrier cover, overlain with rock armour, to minimise both erosion and evaporation of moisture from the radon barrier layer (Olympic Dam Expansion Project Environmental Impact Statement, Kinhill 1997).

The population density is about 0.21 person/km^2 within 100 km, and 1.5 persons/km^2 within a 2 000-km radius (population of Australia) (SENES 1998).

Ranger, Australia

The Ranger mine is located about 220 km east of Darwin in Northern Australia in the Alligator Rivers Region. This district is an area of national and international importance related to tourism, Aboriginal culture and wetland habitat. In 1996/97 the uranium production was about 4 178 t. The average ore grade is about 0.3%.

The tailings contain about 13.9×10^6 t on an area of 107 ha. To prevent environmental degradation all tailings will be returned to worked out pits at the cessation of mining.

The local (100 km) population density around the site is estimated to be 0.054 person/km^2 (local residents and Aboriginal people in the vicinity of the mine). At longer distances (2 000 km) the density is estimated to about 1.8 persons/km^2 (SENES 1998).

Site-specific dose assessments

An estimation of the doses to the local populations through the critical group concept has been performed for the Key Lake/McArthur River facilities in Canada using *e.g.,* the UTAP (Uranium Tailings Assessment Program) and INTAKE model. The UTAP model is a pathway model, which has been set up within a probabilistic framework to assess the movement of contaminants from mining and milling sites. The results are the arithmetic means of 100 trials for the final year of operation, which is predicted to have the highest cumulative dose.

For the calculations, the following pathways were considered: intake of locally harvested food, intake of water, inhalation of dust and radon progeny and ground shine. Fish as well as small and large game were considered as an important part of the diet. The receptors that were considered included operators of fishing lodges located in the neighbourhood of the mine, residents of the mine camp and hunter/gatherer living year-round near the mines.

The estimated doses from all sources (natural background, mine, mill, etc.) ranged from 0.13 mSv at McArthur River to 0.94 mSv for the hunter/gatherer near Key Lake. Key Lake camp workers have been predicted to receive only 27% of their exposure from background, with the majority of the remainder from radon.

Given the high percentage that big game comprises in a person's overall dose, the lichen – caribou-human pathway was especially investigated as a worst case scenario. The dose to a woodland caribou for an area of 332 km² adjacent to Key Lake was modelled. It was assumed that the main uptake pathways for radionuclides were through water and lichen. The predicted dose to a person who ate caribou from this area as their only protein source was estimated to 0.2 mSv/a.

The critical group for Olympic Dam is the residents of Roxby Downs. There are no Aboriginal people living near Olympic Dam. Nor is there any agriculture of any type or surface waters of drainage leading towards human habitation, due to the arid nature of the region. The groundwater is unsuitable for human consumption due to poor quality. Water for the Roxby Downs is pumped from Great Artesian Basin over 100 km away. The exposure pathway that is most critical is inhalation of radon progeny. The effective critical group dose is estimated to about 0.020 mSv/a.

The definition of critical groups for the Ranger mine includes two very different groups. The first group consists of residents of Jabiru, located about eight kilometres west of the mine site. The population of Jabiru is approximately 1 400 comprised predominantly of individuals of European lineage ("western lifestyle"). The majority of the families derive part of their income from the mine. The dominant exposure pathway is inhalation of radon progeny. The water supply is not impacted upon by the mining operations.

The second group consists of Aboriginal residents of Mudginberri station, which is about twelve kilometres from the mine site. Their lifestyle is a blend of European and Aboriginal culture. They consume a mix of traditional «bush» foods and food purchased from the supermarket. A significant proportion of their water intake comes from the surface waters of the Magela Creek. Important pathways are ingestion of radionuclides in the surface water and in "bush" foods.

The average effective dose to the critical groups was estimated to approximately 0.020 mSv (adult) and 0.030 mSv (child) in 1996.

The tailings present a hazard for future generations, which is associated with the radioactive half-lives of the radionuclides involved and stable elements. Computer modelling currently does estimations of various long term health and environmental impacts from uranium mining (UNSCEAR 1993, BIOMOVS Study 1999, SENES 1998, EUR 1995). A major problem in these risk assessments is the selection of appropriate time-periods for the prediction of possible detrimental effects. In addition there seem to be uncertainties regarding possible failures for the waste containment structures which will influence the final results. Therefore modelling results should only be interpreted as indicators of potential impacts and trends, rather than absolute values.

Several studies have been published where long-term population doses have been estimated. In the latest UNSCEAR report 1993, a collective effective dose for abandoned tailing piles is estimated to 150 manSv/GWa for a time period of 10 000 years. However, UNSCEAR stated that the dose could range between 1 and 1 000 manSv/GWa due to the uncertainties in the presumptions.

In a study undertaken by the European Commission on the external costs of the various energy production systems (Dreicer *et al.* 1995), the impact of the extraction and ore processing stages was assessed for the French Lodève site. A collective dose of 0.18 manSv/TWh (1.6 manSv/GWa) was derived but the study was based on the same source term as used in the UNSCEAR-report 1993. A sensitivity analysis for various source terms corresponding to this site has recently been performed (Tort *et al.* 1999). Individual dose for critical persons at 1-2 km away from the site ranged from 0.023 mSv to 0.35 mSv/a and the average dose in the first 10 km was estimated to 0.02 mSv/a. The collective dose was estimated to 360 manSv/GWa, corresponding to a source term of 28 Bq km^2 s^1 without remediation. After remediation, the radon exhalation rate falls down to 0.2 Bq km^2 s^{-1}. This is equal to the local natural background and consequently the collective dose becomes nil.

The study made by SENES Consultants for the Uranium Institute (SENES 1998) is based on gathered information from eight major uranium production facilities that currently (1997) are responsible for 67% of the world's production of uranium. The calculated average dose, accumulated over 10 000 years, was estimated to 0.96 manSv/GWa.

In a newly published report of the BIOMOVS II study (Camus *et al.* 1999), which was established to compare computer models used to assess long term impacts of contaminants released from mill tailings, some generic conclusions about exposure pathways have been drawn. Features that need to be considered in modelling include the tailing chemistry, the engineered barriers, long term degradation effects on engineered barriers and tailing material, the hydrogeological system, the local biosphere and the assessment endpoints. It seems that a range of pathways and contaminants will affect the total dose/intake and that peak impacts on individuals may not arise for maybe hundred years.

Bibliography

BIOMOVS Study 1998, see Camus *et al.* 1999.

CAMUS, H., LITTLE, R. et al, "Long-term contaminate migration and impacts from uranium mill tailings", in *J. Environ. Radio.*, Vol. 42, pp.289-304, 1999 (BIOMOVS Study).

DREICER, M., TORT, V., and MANEN, P., "Nuclear fuel cycle", Report N° 234, ExternE Project, 1995.

EUR (1995), *ExternE Externalities of Energy, Vol. 5: Nuclear*, European Commission Report EUR 16524 EN.

ICRP, "Protection against radon-222 at home and at work", ICRP Publication 65, 1993.

"Long-term population dose due to radon (^{222}Rn) released from uranium mill tailings", SENES Consultants Limited, 1998.

METCALF, P.E., "Management of waste from the mining and milling of uranium and thorium-bearing ores", in *Proceedings IRPA 9, 1996 International Congress on Radiation Protection*, Vienna, pp.1-391.

"Olympic Dam Corporation Environmental Management and Monitoring Report, 1999".

TORT, V., SCHNEIDER, T. and DAROUSSIN, J.-L. (1999), « Évaluation de l'impact radiologique du radon associé au stockage des résidus de traitement de minerais d'uranium » ; in *Radioprotection*, vol. 34, n° 4, pp. 491-504.

UNSCEAR (United Nations Scientific Committee on the Effects of Atomic Radiation), *Sources, effects and risks of ionizing radiation,* UNSCEAR Report 93.

WMC, "WMC Limited Annual Report 1998".

A2. CONVERSION, ENRICHMENT AND FUEL FABRICATION

Reference sites

Experience on discharges from specific plants is provided in the following tables.

Table A1. **Discharges of radionuclides in liquid effluents from BNFL Springfields, 1995-1997**

Radionuclide	Annual discharges (GBq/a)		
	1995	**1996**	**1997**
^{230}Th	5.7×10^1	4.8×10^1	5.2×10^1
^{232}Th	1.6	1.4	1.1
U(•)	4.8×10^1	6.1×10^1	5.7×10^1
^{234}Th*	5.5×10^4	7.5×10^4	7.1×10^4
^{234m}Pa*	5.5×10^4	7.5×10^4	7.1×10^4

* Based on beta measurements of discharge and assumed to consist of 50% ^{234}Th and 50% ^{234}Pa.

Table A2. **Discharges of radionuclides from Malvesi/Pierrelatte conversion facilities**

	Annual discharges			
	Gaseous		Liquid	
	GBq/a	**GBq/GWa**	**GBq/a**	**GBq/GWa**
Malvesi				
^{234}U	1.3×10^{-1}	2.2×10^{-3}	6.4	1.1×10^{-1}
^{235}U	5.5×10^{-3}	9.6×10^{-5}	2.7×10^{-1}	4.8×10^{-3}
^{238}U	1.2×10^{-1}	2.1×10^{-3}	6.0	1.1×10^{-1}
Pierrelatte				
^{234}U	4.6×10^{-2}	1.3×10^{-3}	7.0×10^{-3}	2.0×10^{-4}
^{235}U	2.0×10^{-3}	5.7×10^{-5}	3.0×10^{-4}	8.6×10^{-6}
^{238}U	4.3×10^{-2}	1.2×10^{-3}	6.7×10^{-3}	1.9×10^{-4}

From (EUR 1995) ExternE-Study, Section 5.3.

75

Table A3. **Discharges from the Gronau enrichment plant (1 800 tSWU/a)**

Gaseous discharges via stock	Authorised limit(GBq/a)	Discharges 1997(GBq/a)
α-activity (without Rn-220, 222)	5.2×10^{-3}	2.4×10^{-5}
β-activity	5.2×10^{-3}	1.6×10^{-4}
Liquid discharges	**Authorised limit**	**Discharges 1997**
α-activity	7.4×10^{-4}	3.0×10^{-6}
β-activity	2.8×10^{-3}	2.0×10^{-5}

In addition, very small limits for discharges have been authorised from the enrichment building via building ventilation, and from the storage area for U-feed and U-tails material.

Table A4. **Gaseous releases from the MELOX MOX fuel fabrication plant (1997)**

Radionuclide	Activity released (GBq)	Activity released (GBq/GWa)
^{238}Pu	$< 6.7 \times 10^{-5}$	$< 2.5 \times 10^{-5}$
^{239}Pu, ^{240}Pu	$< 5.8 \times 10^{-5}$	$< 2.1 \times 10^{-5}$

Note: Gaseous effluents are only monitored for plutonium isotopes.
< means "lower than the detection level".

Table A5. **Liquid releases from the MELOX MOX fuel fabrication plant (1997)**

Radionuclide	Activity released (GBq)	Activity released (GBq/GWa)
^{238}Pu	$< 2.0 \times 10^{-3}$	$< 7.3 \times 10^{-4}$
^{239}Pu	$< 3.4 \times 10^{-4}$	$< 1.2 \times 10^{-4}$
^{240}Pu	$< 4.8 \times 10^{-4}$	$< 1.7 \times 10^{-4}$
^{241}Pu	$< 1.7 \times 10^{-6}$	$< 6.0 \times 10^{-7}$
^{242}Pu	$< 1.7 \times 10^{-6}$	$< 6.0 \times 10^{-7}$
^{241}Am	$< 2.9 \times 10^{-4}$	$< 1.0 \times 10^{-4}$
Total α activity	$< 3.0 \times 10^{-3}$	$< 1.1 \times 10^{-3}$

Note: After gross α-measurement, nuclide specific activities are deduced using a reference spectrum. It would not be relevant to quote uranium isotopes activities that are far lower than that of plutonium isotopes, as uranium specific activity is negligible compared to plutonium specific activity.

< means "lower than the detection level".

Table A6. **Occupational doses at EURODIF (1997)**

	Number of workers	Number of workers with doses above zero	Collective dose (manSv)	Individual dose (mSv) distribution			
				0-0.35	0.35-0.75	0.75-1.5	> 1.5
EURODIF workers	1 006	40	0.018	22	13	5	0
Outside workers	614	3	0.001	1	2	0	0
All workers	1 620	43	0.019	23	15	5	0

Bibliography

EUR (1995), *ExternE Externalities of Energy, Vol. 5: Nuclear*, European Commission Report EUR 16524 EN.

HÖRMANN, E. (1996), "Aktualisierung des Sicherheitsvergleichs zwischen Wiederaufarbeitung und Direkter Endlagerung sowie des Kenntnisstandes zur Konditionierung abgebrannter Brennelemente", Unterauftrag zu BMU-Vorhaben SR 2986, August 1996.

A3. POWER GENERATION

Discharges from French PWRs

Figure A1. Annual liquid discharges from French 900 MWe PWR

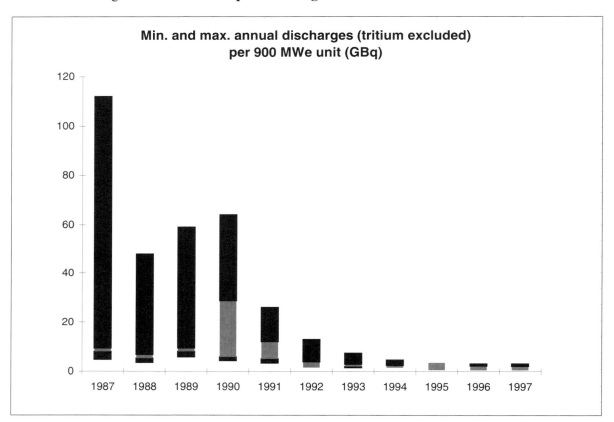

Note: Discharges of plants in which at least one of the reactors is loaded with MOX fuel are in grey.

Figure A2.   **Annual liquid discharges from French 1 300 MWe PWR**

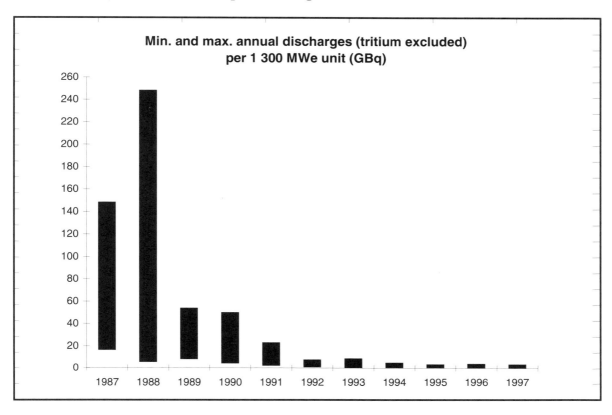

Min. and max. annual discharges (tritium excluded)
per 1 300 MWe unit (GBq)

Table A7.   **Isotopic composition of liquid discharges from two French reactors in 1996**
(except tritium)

	^{54}Mn (%)	^{58}Co (%)	^{60}Co (%)	^{110m}Ag (%)	^{124}Sb (%)	^{131}I (%)	^{134}Cs (%)	^{137}Cs (%)	Others (%)
900-MWe reactor									
Saint-Laurent	1.0	15.0	9.0	43.0	12.0	2.5	2.0	4.0	11.5
1 300-MWe reactor									
Saint-Alban	0.7	34.1	19.1	6.1	8.5	0.3	8.2	19.8	3.1

Plant in which at least one reactor is loaded with MOX fuel.
Predominant nuclide.

Table A8. **Isotopic composition of the discharge gases from two French reactors in 1996**

	Noble gases and tritium*						Halogens and aerosols**						
	Total (TBq)	^{85}Kr (%)	^{133}Xe (%)	^{135}Xe (%)	^{41}Ar (%)	^{3}H (%)	Total (MBq)	^{131}I (%)	^{133}I (%)	^{58}Co (%)	^{60}Co (%)	^{134}Cs (%)	^{137}Cs (%)
900-MWe type reactor													
St-Laurent	1.75	4.7	60.0	7.0	1.9	26.3	20.5	85.6	10.4	0.9	1.1	0.7	0.8
1 300-MWe type reactor													
St-Alban	9.72	0.3	46.3	11.5	1.2	40.8	145.6	69.4	18.8	5.7	2.7	1.8	1.7

> Plant in which at least one reactor is loaded with MOX fuel.

* Other noble gases (mainly ^{85m}Kr, ^{87}Kr, ^{88}Kr, ^{133m}Xe, ^{138}Xe) are not taken into account in the spectrum. Their Activity is estimated at approximately 10% of the total.

** Measurements by γ spectrometry were not carried out in real time, the iodine isotopes with a period of less than 24 h were not calculated. They constitute approximately 50% of the total for iodines.

Table A9. **Change in liquid discharges from two French 900 and 1 300-MWe type reactors**
(Source: EDF 1997)

Year	Saint-Laurent A1-A2 B1-B2 (900 MWe)				Saint-Alban 1-2 (1 300 MWe)			
	Beta total (GBq)	Gamma total (GBq)	Sum R.E. (GBq)	Tritium (TBq)	Beta total (GBq)	Gamma total (GBq)	Sum R.E. (GBq)	Tritium (TBq)
1987	17	58	32	43	88	264	141	29
1988	10	41	21	31	30	165	95	21
1989	18	80	32	43	23	120	65	37
1990	11	58	23	34	25	100	61	30
1991	11	49	20	36	9	53	30	24
1992	8.0	19	6.0	41	2	12	6	9
1993	13	26	8.6	33	1.1	8.6	3.4	13
1994	8.2	16	5.4	24	1.3	6.6	2.8	16
1995	4.8	6.0	2.3	16	1.7	6.7	3.0	22
1996	4.7	6.2	2.0	20	2.2	5.0	3.0	43
1997	3.6	7.1	3.0	17	1.9	8.2	5.4	23

> Plant in which one unit is loaded with MOX fuel.
> Plant in which two units are loaded with MOX fuel.

Liquid discharges – aside from tritium – from French PWRs diminished drastically in the period from 1987 to 1997, as a result of the implementation of new effluent treatment methods, of the staff awareness and training, and of the identification and application of good practices, which made it possible to considerably reduce the difference between the most efficient plants and those with elevated discharges. Radioactive liquid discharges, aside from tritium, have decreased by more than a factor of 10.

Table A10. **Change in gaseous discharges from French 900 MWe and 1300 MWe type reactors**
Source: (EDF 1997)

	Saint-Laurent A1-A2 B1-B2		Saint-Alban Nos. 1-2	
	Gas (TBq)	A+H (GBq)	Gas (TBq)	A+H (GBq)
1987	11	0.15	15	0.10
1988	< 8.6	< 0.10	< 17	< 0.09
1989	< 23	< 0.17	< 10	< 0.12
1990	< 4.7	< 0.09	< 11	< 0.09
1991	< 2.0	< 0.03	< 16	< 0.30
1992	< 8.7	< 0.04	< 14	< 0.12
1993	< 9.2	< 0.04	< 14	< 0.13
1994	< 9.4	< 0.04	< 13	< 0.09
1995	< 19	< 0.08	< 13	< 0.60
1996	< 11	< 0.075	< 11	< 0.14
1997	< 12	< 0.10	< 14	< 0.12

Plant in which one unit is loaded with MOX fuel.
Plant in which two units are loaded with MOX fuel.

A+H: Aerosols and halogens.

Radioactive gaseous discharges comprise planned releases (which are the result of emptying the hold-up tanks) and ventilation system releases. Ventilation system releases (approximately 90%) are always lower than detection thresholds, and thus only an upper bound estimation of the releases is available. This estimation varies according to changes in the detection threshold.

Doses to workers in some NEA Member countries

Table A11. **Normalised annual collective dose to workers (mean 1994-1996)**

	Mean annual collective dose by plant (manSv)	Mean annual collective dose per GW installed manSv/GW(e)	Mean annual collective dose per GWa generated manSv/GWa
United States	1.423	1.39	3.7
Japan	1.221	1.24	1.8
Korea	1.022	1.07	1.2
Asia (mean)	1.155	1.19	1.6
Belgium	1.292	1.31	1.8
France	1.641	1.62	2.4
Germany	1.764	1.44	2.7
Spain	1.783	1.89	2.4
Sweden	0.758	0.80	1.1
Switzerland	1.156	1.17	1.2
Europe (mean)	1.609	1.56	2.3
China	0.684	0.74	1.1
South Africa	0.872	0.90	1.5
Non NEA Member countries (mean)	0.778	0.82	1.3
Total (mean)	1.463	1.43	2.7

Source: NEA Information System on Occupational Exposure (ISOE), (NEA 1996).

Bibliography

EDF (1996), « Électricité de France – Production transport, Département Sécurité Radioprotection Environnement, Résultats Sécurité Radioprotection Incendie 1996 ».

EDF (1997), « Électricité de France – Production transport, Département Sécurité Radioprotection Environnement », Activity Report 1997 – Environment Appendix.

NEA (1996), "OECD Nuclear Energy Agency – International Atomic Energy Agency, Occupational Exposures at Nuclear Power Plants, Sixth Annual Report (1986-1996)".

A4.   REPROCESSING AND VITRIFICATION

Trends over time of discharges of the La Hague 1997 reprocessing plant

From 1987 to 1997, the amount of spent fuel processed has increased by a factor of 4 from 425 tHM to 1 670 tHM.

Over the same period, liquid releases of H3 have increased from 2960 TBq to 11900 TBq, still well below the maximum authorised 37 000 TBq. Other β-γ emitters decreased from 1110 TBq to < 50 TBq, well below the maximum authorised of 1 700 TBq. The activity of caesium and strontium released in 1996 were 7.7 TBq (maximum authorised 220 TBq) and the I129 activity was 1.7 TBq. Total α emitters, 0.46 TBq in 1987, were cut by 10 in 1997, that is 0.045 TBq (maximum authorised 1.7 TBq).

Over the same period, gaseous releases of H3 were 15 TBq in 1987 and increased slowly to 75.7 TBq (maximum authorised 2 200 TBq). I129 increased from 0.015 TBq to 0.036 TBq, ^{85}Kr increased by a factor of 7 from 42 000 TBq to 297 000 TBq (maximum authorised 480 000 TBq). Aerosols were slightly decreasing from 6.10^{-5} TBq in 1987 to 2.10^{-5} TBq in 1996 (maximum authorised 0.074 TBq).

Bibliography

COGEMA (1998), *Dossiers d'enquête publique La Hague, Décembre 1998*, INB 117, COGEMA, p.73; liquid, p.81 gaseous, pp.104-109.

A5.   INTERIM STORAGE AND CONDITIONING OF SPENT FUEL

Reference sites

Table A12.   **Discharges from CLAB in 1996**

Radionuclides	Discharged activities (Bq)	
	To air	**To water**
^{3}H		2.7×10^9
^{22}Na		8.8×10^4
^{51}Cr		4.2×10^6
^{54}Mn	3.3×10^5	1.2×10^7
^{57}Co		2.3×10^5
^{58}Co		8.6×10^6
^{60}Co	2.8×10^7	4.2×10^8
^{59}Fe		8.4×10^5
^{65}Zn		3.6×10^6
^{90}Sr	8.1×10^4	2.9×10^5
^{110m}Ag		1.4×10^6
^{124}Sb		4.3×10^5
^{125}Sb	2.4×10^5	2.4×10^7
^{134}Cs		4.2×10^6
^{137}Cs		8.8×10^7
^{140}La		1.3×10^5
^{239}Pu/^{240}Pu		8.5×10^2
^{238}Pu/^{241}Am		3.2×10^4
^{243}Cm/^{244}Cm		1.0×10^4
^{242}Cm		4.9×10^3
^{243}Am		3.6×10^3

From these releases doses to the critical group (site-specific) in 1996 were estimated to be 1.2×10^{-6} mSv for gaseous discharges and 4.0×10^{-6} mSv for liquid discharges.

Table A13. **Design basis radioactive discharges for
Paks interim spent fuel storage facility according to the safety case**

Isotopes	Gaseous discharges (Bq/a)		Liquid discharges (Bq/a)
	Via chimney	Charge hall	
^{3}H	5.4×10^{7}		3.1×10^{7}
^{54}Mn	2.3×10^{5}	9.0×10^{3}	1.1×10^{4}
^{60}Co	6.4×10^{5}	2.5×10^{4}	1.8×10^{4}
^{110m}Ag	6.4×10^{4}	2.5×10^{3}	1.1×10^{6}
Other β/γ fission or activation products	< 1		1.9×10^{5}
α nuclides	$< 5 \times 10^{-5}$		2.0×10^{2}

The practical experience with loading of 450 irradiated fuel assemblies during start-up of the storage facility in Paks in 1997 shows that real discharges are far less in comparison to the design basis values of the safety case. Due to some problems in connection with active commissioning of the facility the ^{3}H gaseous discharges were slightly higher than anticipated. In the case of gaseous discharges other than tritium, only ^{54}Mn, ^{60}Co and ^{110m}Ag could be measured. All other radionuclides were below the detection limits. The liquid discharges of ^{54}Mn and ^{60}Co exceeded the design basis values by a factor of 4 to 6, the ^{3}H discharge was far less than the design value.

Table A14. **Pilot conditioning facility Gorleben: Proposed maximum discharges in the safety case**

Radionuclides	Proposed maximum discharges in application (Bq/a)	
	Gaseous	Liquid
^{3}H	7.4×10^{11}	3.7×10^{8}
^{85}Kr	1.5×10^{15}	
^{129}I	8.1×10^{7}	
α aerosols	6.7×10^{7}	7.4×10^{7}
β/γ aerosols	4.4×10^{9}	1.9×10^{9}

Resulting maximum individual doses for the population have been calculated according to these values in the application (0.004 mSv/a whole body dose, 0.031 mSv/a thyroid dose). No licence has been issued for this project up to now.

In (Hörmann 1996) a collective dose of 6×10^{-5} manSv/GWa for the population has been assessed for this stage of conditioning spent fuel assemblies.

Bibliography

HÖRMANN, E. (1996), "Aktualisierung des Sicherheitsvergleichs zwischen Wiederaufarbeitung und Direkter Endlagerung sowie des Kenntnisstandes zur Konditionierung abgebrannter Brennelemente", Unterauftrag zu BMU-Vorhaben SR 2986, August 1996.

A6. TRANSPORTATION

Reference data

Concerning the radiological impact from the normal transport operations of radioactive material within the nuclear fuel cycle, mostly fragmentary data are available in the literature. Some countries do have detailed information but most countries do not. The most comprehensive data source constituted by an IAEA technical committee (IAEA 1986). The relevant data are shown in Table A15. Although the data were incomplete, insofar as they do not represent a global set, and are restricted in some cases to only part of the transport field in the countries, it could be concluded from this report that exposures from normal transport operations are very low both for workers and for members of the public. UNSCEAR, in its 1988 report (UNSCEAR 1988) derived normalised collective effective dose equivalents of 0.2 manSv/GWa and 0.1 manSv/GWa, for the occupational and population exposure respectively, from the submissions of the United States and the United Kingdom to the IAEA study. In the UNSCEAR report of 1993 (UNSCEAR 1993) the normalised collective effective dose value of 0.1 manSv/GWa for the population was confirmed.

At present, the best-documented data concerning doses from transport of radioactive material in Europe originate from France, the UK and Germany. All three countries reprocess spent fuel, which is carried out in France or in the UK The dose values are indicated in Table A16. Only transport in normal conditions (routine operations) are considered. In Finland, where reprocessing is not applied, VTT Energy has recently carried out a comprehensive analysis of health risks brought about by transportation of spent fuel (Suolanen *et al.* 1999). The results are also indicated in Table A16.

The French data originate from dose estimations to the workers and the public on a triennial basis from 1981 to 1990 (Hammard *et al.* 1993). In a French-German study (Fett *et al.* 1997) dose assessments are reported concerning the return of reprocessing waste material from France (La Hague) to Germany (Gorleben). This waste originates from the reprocessing of 4 650 tHM from the German electricity production from 1985 to 1995. In a German study (Schneider *et al.* 1984) about waste disposal for a once-through cycle is reported. The radiological dose and risk from the transport of spent fuel and low-level waste corresponding with 700 tHM annually for a nuclear energy production of 26.6 GW(e) is evaluated. In (Gelder 1992) results of dose assessments were reported for the normal transport of radioactive materials within the UK up to the year 1989. In (Hörmann 1996) a dose comparison is made between the two nuclear fuel cycles considered for the German situation.

From the data in Tables A15 and A16, normalised collective doses (per unit of electricity produced in the nuclear power plants) have been calculated, taking into account the nuclear electricity productions in the corresponding years, in the countries concerned (Table A17). However since the years during which the transport of spent fuel and wastes takes place, may not correspond to the years, during which this fuel has produced electricity, there is some inaccuracy in the results. The normalised collective doses have been divided between transport of fresh fuel or of separated uranium and recovered plutonium, transport of spent fuel and transport of wastes.

For spent fuel, the dose values are not too different from each other, except for the values in Finland. Differences between occupational doses may be due to the distances to be covered and to the transport conditions. Collective doses to the public also depend heavily on the population and traffic density. However the French and UK data may include shipments of foreign fuel, which lead to an overestimation of doses, except for the lowest values of the public doses in the UK (1989), where only UK fuel was included. The reason for the high Finnish dose values, especially to the workers, is related to the highly conservative assumptions and inclusion of extreme scenarios. Concerning the differences in transport doses between the two options considered, it is obvious that they are mainly associated with the locations of the facilities for conditioning and for reprocessing. The quantities of spent fuel per unit quantity of energy produced, will not differ much between the options.

For transportation of fresh fuel or of separated uranium and recovered plutonium, possible reasons for differences between the reported values are roughly the same as for the transport of spent fuel. There may be some differences in collective doses between the two options considered, notwithstanding the fact that the same quantities of fuel are needed for the same production of electricity. The transport of separated uranium and recovered plutonium from the reprocessing facility to the fuel fabrication plant is likely to bring about a lower dose than the transport of an equivalent quantity of ore from uranium mines, which is still to be transported to the conversion and enrichment plant before the transport to the fuel fabrication plant. In most cases it can be expected that transport labour and conditions will be in favour (bringing about a lower dose) of the transport of fuel from the reprocessing facilities. No specific values for the transport of uranium to the enrichment and fuel fabrication plants have been collected. Yet the difference between the two options, in terms of total dose, may not be large, the quantity of uranium ore needed for the fabrication of fresh fuel being not very different between both cycles.

With respect to the transport of radioactive waste within the nuclear fuel cycle, distinction has to be made between the (intermediate and low-level) wastes from nuclear power plants (NPP) and the wastes originating from reprocessing and from conditioning facilities. Whilst it is not expected that the transport dose associated with the waste from the NPP will differ considerably between the two options, more important differences may occur for the wastes from the other two facility types. In the literature, doses from transportation of ILW and LLW, are mostly not detailed as to their origin (NPP, reprocessing, conditioning). Only the German and French-German data collected in (Fett *et al.* 1997) and (Schneider *et al.* 1984), are detailed enough to make this distinction. From those data, a difference of the order of 2×10^{-3} manSv/GWa in total collective dose (to workers and public) may be derived in favour of the once-through cycle, if the intermediate and low-level waste from NPPs are not taken into account. They may be explained partly by the larger distance to the reprocessing facility (La Hague) than to the conditioning facility (in southern Germany) with respect to the disposal site (Gorleben). Also, the quantities of ILW and LLW are expected to be larger for the reprocessing option because of the contributions from the reprocessing stage. As to the transport of high-level waste (including irradiated fuel) from conditioning and from reprocessing, the total collective doses (to public and workers) reported in the same studies are quite similar for the two options. The quantity of HLW to be transported is however smaller in the case of reprocessing, but this will be balanced by the larger transportation distance for the closed fuel cycle.

When considering routine transportation of radioactive materials in the three important segments of the nuclear fuel cycle, namely spent fuel, fresh fuel and waste, the differences in normalised collective doses (both occupational and public) between the two considered fuel cycle options are expected to be relatively small; of the order of some 10^{-3} manSv/GWa. The differences may be brought about, on the one hand by the location of the installations, on the other hand by factors that are inherent to the systems. These factors may include the larger amounts of fresh uranium ore and spent fuel to be transported in the once-through cycle, and the larger amounts of LLW and ILW and separated uranium and recovered plutonium in the reprocessing option. A recent German study (Hörmann 1996) however indicates larger collective doses for the closed cycle with differences of the order of more than 10^{-2} man Sv/GWa for the occupational dose and of an order of magnitude lower for the dose to the public. The figures of the occupational dose are in contradiction with the figures for Germany in the IAEA report (IAEA 1986), but correspond with the figure for the UK in the same document. A Finnish study summarised in (Suolanen *et al.* 1999) however indicates high occupational dose values (up to the order of the values for the whole fuel cycle in Germany) for the transport of spent fuel only in a once-through fuel cycle.

The maximum annual individual doses reported range from trivial ones to the public (less than 0.01 or 0.03 mSv/a) to less than 5 mSv/a (10 mSv/a for Finland) for the workers in Europe.

To conclude with, it has to be stressed that the radiological impact from transportation depends on a number of factors: the material transported and its radioactivity, distance and mode of transportation, location of facilities, and population distribution. In addition to these complexity and fragmented data, no generic model has been found to be suitable for systematic comparison of radiological impact of two options.

Bibliography

FETT, H.-J. LANGE, F. Lombard, J. *et al.,* "Transport risk assessment study for reprocessing waste materials to be returned from France to Germany. IPSN, CEPN, GRS Final Report", GRS – 141, Gesellschaft für Anlagen- und Reaktorsicherheit (GRS) mbH, Cologne, 1997.

GELDER, R., "Radiation Exposure from the normal transport of radioactive materials with the United Kingdom. 1991 Review", NRPB-R255, National Radiological Protection Board, Chilton, Didcot, 1992.

HAMMARD, J., RINGOT, C. *et al.,* "Estimation of the individual and collective doses received by workers and the public during the transport of radioactive materials", *Transport of Radioactive Materials (PATRAM),* Vol. 1, 67-73, Yokohama, 1993.

HÖRMANN, E. (1996), "Aktualisierung des Sicherheitsvergleichs zwischen Wiederaufarbeitung und Direkter Endlagerung sowie des Kenntnisstandes zur Konditionierung abgebrannter Brenn-elemente. Unterauftrag zu BMU-Vorhaben SR 2986, August 1996.

IAEA (1986), "Assessment of the radiological impact of the transport of radioactive materials", International Atomic Energy Agency, IAEA-TECDOC-398, Vienna.

POSIVA (1999), "The final disposal facility of spent nuclear fuel – Environmental impact assessment report, Main Report", Posiva Oy, Helsinki, 1999.

SCHNEIDER, K. JOBST, C. *et al.,* "Technisches Konzept und Sicherheitsanalyse des Transports von Endlagergebinden mit abgebrannten Brennelementen", Anschlussbericht, Technischer Anhang 5, KWA 3302/0, KWA 3310/7 in *Andere Entsorgungstechniken. F+E Schwerpunkt des Bundesministerium für Forschung und Technologie.,* Transnuklear GmbH, NUKEM GmbH, Hanau, 1984.

SUOLANEN, V., VUORI, S. and PÖLLÄNEN, L. "Risk analysis of spent fuel transportation related to EIA for repository site evaluation", *Nuclear Europe Worldscan,* (1999) Nos. 5-6, pp. 42-43.

UNSCEAR (1988), United Nations Scientific Committee on the Effects of Atomic Radiation (UNSCEAR), *Sources, Effects and Risks of Ionizing Radiation, 1988, Report to the General Assembly, with annexes,* United Nations, New York, 1988.

UNSCEAR (1993), United Nations Scientific Committee on the Effects of Atomic Radiation (UNSCEAR), *Sources and Effects of Ionizing Radiation, 1993, Report to the General Assembly, with annexes,* United Nations, New York, 1993.

Table A15. **Radiological impact from transport in the nuclear fuel cycle (IAEA 1986)**

Country	Products	Public exposure		Occupational exposure		Type of transport	
		Individual (mSv/a)	Collective (manSv)	Individual (mSv/a)	Collective (manSv)	Road	Rail
FRG 1983	Fresh and spent fuel, UF$_6$, ores and wastes		0.019 (A)[1]	0.06 (A)	0.018 (A)		All
Finland 1982, 1985	Spent fuel		0.0006-0.0014 (A)	0.2-0.5 (M)[2]	0.0004-0.001 (A)	13 km	230 km
France 1982-85	Irradiated fuel			0.5-1.1 (M)	0.007-0.026 (M)	All	
1982-85	Low-level waste			1.7-3.7 (M)	0.040-0.047 (M)	All	
1983-85	Pu and enriched U			0.07-0.18 (M)	0.007-0.018 (M)	All	
1982-85	Other radioactive materials			0.03-0.6 (M)	0.0016-0.093 (M)	All	
Italy 1981	Fuel elements (PWR)		0.01 (A)	0.03 (M)	0.01 (M)	700 km	
Sweden 1975-85	Spent and fresh fuel, low-level waste			0.04 (M)	0.002 (M, A)	All	
UK 1981	All radioactive materials in the nuclear fuel cycle			0.1 (M, A)	0.14 (M, A)	Both	Both
	Irradiated fuel	0.002 max. (A)	0.001 (A)			Both	Both
USA 1985	All radioactive materials in the nuclear fuel cycle	0.02 max. (A)	19 (A)	9 max. (M)	19 (M,A)	All modes	All modes

A = Assessed.
M = Measured.

Table A16. **Radiological impact from transport in the nuclear fuel cycle (other studies)**

Country	Products	Public exposure		Occupational exposure		Type of transport	
		Individual (mSv/a)	Collective (manSv)	Individual (mSv/a)	Collective (manSv)	Road	Rail
France 1981 1986 1990[4]	Irradiated fuel		Maximum: ½ × occupational dose	0.4 (A) 0.6 (A) 0.65 (A)	0.006 (A) 0.01 (A) 0.007 (A)		Mainly
1981 1986 1990	Waste		Maximum: ½ × occupational dose	3.3 (A) 2.8 (A) 1 (A)	0.04 (A) 0.08 (A) 0.03 (A)		Mainly
1981 1986 1990	Other radioactive materials		Maximum: ½ × occupational dose	0.1 (A) 0.4 (A) 0.24 (A)	0.002 (A) 0.009 (A) 0.004 (A)		
France-Germany 1985-95[5]	VHLW from spent fuel	< 0.01	0.005 (A)	< 0.1	0.002 (A)		Mainly
	ILW (sludges)	0.03	0.020 (A)	0.7-1.7	$0.014^{(1)}$ (A)		Mainly
Germany[6]	Spent fuel from NPP	< 0.001	$0.10 + 0.03^{(2)(3)}$	max. 2.5-5	$0.10 + 0.03^{(2)\,(3)}$		
	LLW from NPP	< 0.001	$0.62 + 0.035^{(2)(3)}$	max. 2.5-5	$0.62 + 0.035^{(2)\,(3)}$		
	LLW from conditioning		$0.041^{(2)}$		$0.041^{\,2)}$		
	HLW from conditioning		$0.012^{(2)}$		$0.012^{(2)}$		
UK[7] 1982	Spent fuel		0.0008 (A)		0.005 (A)	All	All
1989	Spent fuel		0.0007 (UK) (A) 0.0023 (import.)	< 0.05-1.2 (road) 0.04 (A)	0.012 (A) (A)	All Rail	All
	Waste			0.026-0.4 (A)	0.014 (A)	All	All
	Other radioactive materials non-irradiated material		$0.024^{(4)}$ (A)		0.005 (A)	Road All	All
	All radioactive materials in the nuclear fuel cycle	0.006 max. 0.004 max.				Road	Rail
Finland[9]	Spent fuel	0.02 max.	0.005-0.014	$0.9\text{-}4.6^{(5)}$ $2.8\text{-}9.8^{(6)}$	$0.009\text{-}0.046^{(5)}$ $0.014\text{-}0.049^{(6)}$		

1. Loading personnel: 2×0.013.
2. Total collective dose (public + occupational for nuclear power of 26.6 GWa.
3. First value = by rail; second value = by road (mainly turnover railroad).
4. Except spent fuel.
5. Crew and convoy.
6. Handlers of casks.

A = Assessed.
M = Measured.

References: [4] (Hammard 1993), [5] (Fett 1997), [6] (Schneider 1984), [7] (Gelder 1992), [9] (Suolanen 1999).

Table A17. Normalised collective doses from transport in the nuclear fuel cycle

	Occupational collective dose (10^{-3} manSv/GWa)			Collective dose to the public (10^{-3} man Sv/GWa)		
	France	United Kingdom	Germany (+ Finland)	France	United Kingdom	Germany (+ Finland)
Spent fuel	0.6-1.7 (1982-85) 0.5 (1981) 0.4 (1986) 0.2 (1990)	1.1 (1982) 1.6 (1989)	4.9[1] Finland: 5.4-22 [9]	Maximum: ½ occupat. dose Idem	0.3 (1981) 0.2 (1982) 0.1 (1989)	4.9[1] Finland: 1.2-3.3[9]
Non-irradiated fuel	0.45-1.4[2] (1982-85) 0.2[3] (1981) 0.3[3] (1986) 0.1[3] (1990)	0.7 (1989)		Maximum: ½ occupat. dose Idem		
	0.2-4.7[4] (1982-85) 3.5 (1981) 2.9 (1986) 0.9 (1990)	1.9 (1989)	From NPP: 25[1] From condit.: 1.5[1] From reproc.: 2.5[5]	Maximum: ½ occupat. dose Idem	3.3[5] (1989)	From NPP: 25[1] From condit.: 1.5[1] From reprocess:1.2[5]
HL waste			From condit.: 0.45[1] From reproc.:0.12[5]			From condit.: 0.45[1] From reproc.: 0.31[5]
ALL	36 (1981)		2.4 (1983)			2.5 (1983)
Once- through			11 [8]			1.3 [8]
Closed cycle			28 [8]			2.9 [8]

1. Occupational + public dose – assumed energy production: 26.6 GWa ([6]).
2. Enriched uranium and plutonium.
3. Possibly other radioactive material included.
4. Low-level radioactive waste.
5. Not only waste.

References: [5] (Fett 1997], [6] (Schneider 1984), [8] (Hörmann 1996), [9] (Suolanen 1999)

Annex B

GENERIC DOSE ASSESSMENT OF THE NUCLEAR FUEL CYCLE

Table of contents

B1. Introduction 95
B2. Input data and Methodology 95
B3. Results of the Generic Assessment 97
B4. Bibliography... 97

List of figures

Figure B1. Modelling of uranium mining and mill tailings heap 98

List of tables

Table B1. Gaseous discharges from mill tailings 98
Table B2. Gaseous and liquid discharges from fuel conversion, enrichment and fabrication..... 98
Table B3. Gaseous and liquid discharges from a typical PWR 99
Table B4. Gaseous and liquid discharges from a typical reprocessing plant............................. 100
Table B5. General Modelling Data.. 101
Table B6. Critical Group Intake Data... 101
Table B7. Occupancy Data.. 102
Table B8. Typical activity concentrations in freshwater bodies close
          to uranium mining facilities 102
Table B9. Critical group doses in the 50th year following 50 years continuous gaseous
          discharges, from mill tailings.. 102
Table B10. Critical group doses from the intake of contaminated drinking water
          and freshwater fish in the vicinity of mill tailings 102
Table B11. Critical group doses in the 50th year following 50 years of continuous gaseous
          discharges, from fuel fabrication and enrichment – Adults 103
Table B12. Critical group doses in the 50th year following 50 years of continuous gaseous
          discharges, from fuel fabrication and enrichment – Infants...................... 103
Table B13. Critical group doses in the 50th year following 50 years of continuous
          liquid discharges, from fuel fabrication and enrichment – Adults............. 104
Table B14. Critical group doses in the 50th year following 50 years of continuous
          liquid discharges, from fuel fabrication and enrichment – Infants 104
Table B15. Critical group doses in the 50th year following 50 years of continuous
          gaseous discharges from a typical coastal PWR – Adults 105
Table B16. Critical group doses in the 50th year following 50 years of continuous
          gaseous discharges from a typical coastal PWR – Infants........................ 106
Table B17. Critical group doses in the 50th year following 50 years of continuous
          gaseous discharges from a typical inland PWR – Adults 107

Table B18. Critical group doses in the 50th year following 50 years of continuous
gaseous discharges from a typical inland PWR – Infants 108

Table B19. Critical group doses in the 50th year following 50 years of continuous
liquid discharges from a typical coastal PWR – Adults... 109

Table B20. Critical group doses in the 50th year following 50 years of continuous
liquid discharges from a typical coastal PWR – Infants 109

Table B21. Critical group doses in the 50th year following 50 years continuous
liquid discharges from a typical Inland PWR – Adults 110

Table B22. Critical group doses in the 50th year following 50 years continuous
liquid discharges from a typical Inland PWR – Infants... 110

Table B23. Critical group doses in the 50th year following 50 years continuous
gaseous discharges from a typical reprocessing plant – Adults................................. 111

Table B24. Critical group doses in the 50th year following 50 years continuous
gaseous discharges from a typical reprocessing plant – Infants 112

Table B25. Critical group doses in the 50th year following 50 years continuous
liquid discharges from a typical reprocessing plant – Adults 113

Table B26. Critical group doses in the 50th year following 50 years continuous
liquid discharges from a typical reprocessing plant – Infants................................... 114

Table B27. Collective doses from mill tailings normalised to GWa generated
truncated at 500 years (Population density 1 person/km^2)... 114

Table B28. Collective doses from mill tailings normalised to GWa generated
truncated at 500 years: Food chain pathways 115

Table B29. Collective doses to the population of Europe truncated at 500 years
following gaseous discharges from fuel fabrication and enrichment......................... 115

Table B30. Collective doses to the population of Europe truncated at 500 years
following liquid releases from fuel fabrication and enrichment 115

Table B31. Collective doses to the population of Europe truncated at 500 years following
gaseous discharges from a typical coastal PWR – Normalised to GWa generated 116

Table B32. Collective doses to the population of Europe truncated at 500 years following
gaseous discharges from a typical inland PWR – Normalised at GWa generated...... 117

Table B33. Collective doses to the population of Europe truncated at 500 years following
liquid releases from a typical coastal PWR – Normalised at GWa generated 118

Table B34. Collective doses to the population of Europe truncated at 500 years following
liquid releases from a typical inland PWR – Normalised at GWa generated 118

Table B35. Collective doses to the population of Europe truncated at 500 years, following
gaseous discharges from a typical reprocessing plant – Normalised at GWa
generated... 119

Table B36. Collective doses to the population of Europe truncated at 500 years, following
liquid discharges from a typical reprocessing plant – Normalised at GWa
generated from UO_2 fuel only 120

B1. Introduction

Critical group doses and collective doses normalised to unit of electricity production have been calculated for the nuclear fuel cycle. For assessment purposes the fuel cycle has been divided into four separate stages, they are: (a) uranium mining and milling, (b) conversion and enrichment and fuel fabrication, (c) power production and finally, (d) reprocessing. In order to simplify the comparisons of each stage of the fuel cycle a standard or generic set of assessment assumptions has been made, including the definition of generic critical groups. Collective doses were also calculated and are presented as normalised to electricity production (*i.e., mansievert per gigawatt-year*). In this way the radiological impact of each stage of the fuel cycle can be compared on similar terms.

B2. Input data and Methodology

The dose assessments were undertaken using PC CREAM 98 [Mayall 1997] and BIOS [Martin 1991]. PC CREAM 98 is a software package for the assessment of routine and continuous discharges of radionuclides to atmosphere, and to marine environments. PC CREAM was developed by the NRPB under contract to the European Commission DGXI. The package is an implementation of the models and methods detailed in European Commission Radiation Protection 72 report: "Methodology for assessing the radiological consequences of routine releases of radionuclides to the environment" [Simmonds 1995]. BIOS is the NRPB biosphere transport model capable of modelling discharges of radionuclides to rivers and the subsequent calculation of collective doses.

The sites chosen for the assessment and the corresponding discharges of radionuclides to the environment are described in Chapter 3 of the main report. These data are summarised in Tables B1 to B4 of this annex.

Data for the mining and milling assessment were based on Canadian and Australian mines, whilst data for the fuel fabrication and enrichment were provided by the UK. The power production stage of the cycle is taken to be representative of discharges from a typical PWR and as such was based on data from French PWR reactors. The dose assessment for reprocessing was taken to be typical of discharges from Cap de la Hague, France. For both discharges to the atmosphere and to the marine environment, two types of doses were calculated: critical group doses (*i.e.*, doses representative of the highest that may be received), and collective doses which are the summed doses to all the individuals in an exposed population.

The term "dose" in this report refers to the effective dose and is the sum of the annual external effective dose and the committed effective dose from intakes over 1 year integrated to 50 years for adults and to 70 years for infants. Doses were determined in accordance with the most recent recommendations of the International Commission on Radiological Protection (ICRP), namely effective dose as defined in ICRP Publication 60 [ICRP 1990] and the dose coefficients presented in ICRP Publication 72 [ICRP 1996]. The individual doses represent the dose an individual would receive in the 50th year following continuous discharges at the same level for 50 years. The collective doses presented are for a single year's discharge truncated at 500 years, rather than integrated to infinity.

Discharges to atmosphere.

For the calculation of doses from discharge to atmosphere PC CREAM uses a standard gaussian plume dispersion model. A uniform windrose meteorological data file, set up to represent 60% Pasquill category D conditions was used to represent meteorological conditions at all of the sites in this assessment. A single stack of 30-m effective release height was used for all but the mining and milling stages of the assessment. The venting of radon from mill tailings was represented by five stacks set at equal distances to represent an idealised heap of tailings, the central stack having an effective release height of 30 m, whilst the four outer stacks were set to 10 m. The area of the tailing heap was taken to be 100 ha ($1 \times 10^6 \, m^2$), see Figure B1. General assumptions used in calculating doses from releases to atmosphere are given in Table B5.

In all cases the critical group was defined as living at a distance of 1 km from the atmospheric discharge point. With the exception of uranium mining and milling, critical group doses were calculated for the following exposure pathways: inhalation of the plume, external exposure from radionuclides in the plume and deposited on the ground, ingestion of terrestrial foodstuffs (see Table B5), and inhalation of resuspended material. Critical group doses for uranium mining and milling were estimated for inhalation of ^{222}Rn only; it was assumed that the area immediately surrounding the facility was unlikely to support extensive production of terrestrial foodstuffs.

The critical group food intake rates are given in Table B6, and were taken from information supplied by Germany and from Robinson 1996. The intakes of milk and root vegetables were assumed to be taken entirely from a reference production point 1 km from the discharge point, whilst 50% of the intake of the remaining foods were taken from 1 km. The other 50% of the intake were assumed to be from locations unaffected by the discharge. Adults were assumed to spend 30% of their time outside whilst infants were assumed to spend only 10% see Table B7.

The assessment of collective doses from atmospheric discharges made use of actual population and agricultural distribution data for Europe for all but the mining and milling stage. The assessment took account of the same exposure pathways as were considered for critical group doses. Where appropriate, the contributions from global circulation of radionuclides were included. For the assessment of collective doses from mining and milling a uniform density population grid representing 1 person/km^2 was produced to give results for two separate distance bands, from 0 to 100 km and from 100 to 2 000 km. Such separation will enable the impact of various population density patterns to be assessed. In this way, collective doses were calculated for inhalation of ^{222}Rn. However, it is possible that doses could also be delivered via food chain pathways following deposition of daughter radionuclides of ^{222}Rn onto soils and crops. The significance of this route of population exposure will depend upon the agricultural productivity of the surrounding region. In the absence of detailed information on this, an upper estimate of the collective doses from food chain pathways was obtained by assuming the release occurred from a site in England using European agricultural production data.

Discharges to the marine environment.

Details of the radionuclide discharges from each stage of the fuel cycle are given in Tables B1 to B4. For discharges directly into the marine environment PC CREAM 98 was used whilst discharges to rivers were modelled using BIOS. For discharges to the marine environment, doses via the following exposure pathways were calculated: ingestion of fish, crustaceans and molluscs; external exposure from occupancy of beaches; and inhalation of sea spray. In the case of discharges to freshwater systems doses from ingestion of fish and drinking water, and from occupancy of riverbanks were estimated together with those arising from the use of river water for irrigation. In estimating critical group doses for discharges to the marine environment, all intakes of seafood were taken from the local marine compartment. Pathways involving inhalation of sea spray and external exposure from beach materials were also assumed to originate in the local marine compartment. For discharges to freshwater, except for uranium mining and milling, all freshwater fish and drinking water intakes were taken from the first river compartment downstream of the discharge point. For the uranium mining and milling calculations, the typical concentrations of radionuclides measured in freshwater bodies near uranium mining facilities were taken (see Table B8). Details of the intake rates are provided in

Table B6, whilst river bank and beach occupancy rates are given in Table B7. In estimating collective doses, calculated concentrations of radionuclides in environmental materials were combined with estimates of seafood catches and of coastline lengths (Simmonds 1995).

B3.   Results of the Generic Assessment

Critical group doses for each stage of the fuel cycle are presented in Tables B9 to B26. Doses are broken down by radionuclide and pathway. Collective doses normalised to electricity production are presented in Tables B27 to B36.

B4.   Bibliography

ICRP, "1990 Recommendations of the International Commission on Radiological Protection", ICRP Publication 60, Annals of the ICRP, 21, Nos. 1-3 (1991).

ICRP, "Age-dependent doses to members of the public from intakes of radionuclides: Part 5 Compilation of ingestion and inhalation dose coefficients", ICRP Publication 72, Annals of the ICRP, Vol. 26, No. 1 (1996).

MAYALL, A. *et al.,* "PC CREAM User Guide", NRPB-SR296, EUR 17791. 1997.

MARTIN, J.S., BARRACLOUGH, I.M. *et al.,* "User guide for BIOS_3A", Chilton, NRPB-M285, (1991).

ROBINSON, C.A., "Generalised habit data for radiological assessments", Chilton, NRPB-M636, (1996).

SIMMONDS, J.R., LAWSON, G. and MAYALL, A., "Methodology for assessing the radiological consequences of routine releases of radionuclides to the environment", Luxembourg, European Community, EUR 15760 (1995).

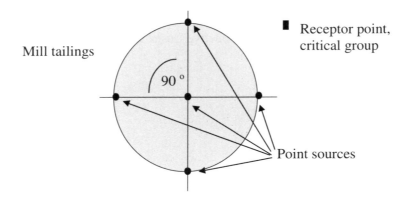

Figure B1. **Modelling of uranium mining and mill tailings heap**

Table B1. **Gaseous discharges from mill tailings**

Radionuclide	Release rate (Bq m^{-2} s^{-1})	Normalised release rate (Bq m^{-2} s^{-1}/GWa)
^{222}Rn	3	3×10^{-2}

Table B2. **Gaseous and liquid discharges from fuel conversion, enrichment and fabrication**

Radionuclide	Discharges (GBq/a^{-1})		Normalised discharges (GBq/GWa)	
	Gaseous	Liquid	Gaseous	Liquid
^{230}Th	Not discharged	5.20×10^{1}	Not discharged	1.49
^{232}Th	Not discharged	1.10	Not discharged	4.00×10^{-2}
^{234}Th	Not discharged	1.44×10^{5}	Not discharged	4.11×10^{3}
^{234}U	5.70×10^{-1}	5.50×10^{1}	1.63×10^{-2}	1.57

Table B3. **Gaseous and liquid discharges from a typical PWR**

Radionuclide	Discharges (GBq/a)		Normalised discharges (GBq/GWa)	
	Gaseous	Liquid	Gaseous	Liquid
^{3}H	9.00×10^2	1.75×10^4	8.41×10^2	1.64×10^4
^{14}C	2.15×10^2	1.61×10^1	2.01×10^2	1.50×10^1
^{41}Ar	3.50×10^1	Not discharged	3.27×10^1	Not discharged
^{54}Mn	Not discharged	1.50×10^{-2}	Not discharged	1.40×10^{-2}
^{58}Co	1.70×10^{-4}	3.65×10^{-1}	1.59×10^{-4}	3.41×10^{-1}
^{60}Co	6.50×10^{-6}	1.65×10^{-1}	6.07×10^{-6}	1.54×10^{-1}
^{63}Ni	Not discharged	3.96×10^{-1}	Not discharged	3.69×10^{-1}
^{85}Kr	6.50	Not discharged	6.07	Not discharged
^{88}Kr	2.30×10^{-1}	Not discharged	2.15×10^{-1}	Not discharged
^{110m}Ag	Not discharged	9.50×10^{-2}	Not discharged	8.88×10^{-2}
^{124}Sb	Not discharged	5.00×10^{-2}	Not discharged	4.67×10^{-2}
^{131}I	1.55×10^{-2}	1.50×10^{-2}	1.45×10^{-2}	1.40×10^{-2}
^{133}I	2.00×10^{-3}	Not discharged	1.87×10^{-3}	Not discharged
^{133}Xe	5.00	Not discharged	4.67	Not discharged
^{134}Cs	ND	6.00×10^{-2}	Not discharged	5.61×10^{-2}
^{137}Cs	ND	1.75×10^{-1}	Not discharged	1.64×10^{-1}

Table B4. **Gaseous and liquid discharges from a typical reprocessing plant**

Radionuclide	Discharges (GBq/a)		Normalised discharges (GBq/GWa)	
	Gaseous	Liquid	Gaseous	Liquid
^{3}H	7.57×10^{4}	1.19×10^{7}	1.67×10^{3}	2.62×10^{5}
^{14}C	1.70×10^{4}	9.65×10^{3}	3.75×10^{2}	2.13×10^{2}
^{54}Mn	Not discharged	4.81×10^{1}	Not discharged	1.06
^{57}Co	Not discharged	1.37	Not discharged	3.02×10^{-2}
^{58}Co	Not discharged	1.64×10^{1}	Not discharged	3.62×10^{-1}
^{60}Co	Not discharged	4.85×10^{2}	Not discharged	1.07×10^{1}
^{63}Ni	Not discharged	1.30×10^{2}	Not discharged	2.86
^{65}Zn	Not discharged	1.68×10^{2}	Not discharged	3.71×10^{-2}
^{85}Kr	2.97×10^{8}	Not discharged	6.55×10^{6}	Not discharged
^{89}Sr	Not discharged	3.73×10^{1}	Not discharged	8.23×10^{-1}
^{90}Sr	Not discharged	3.73×10^{3}	Not discharged	8.23×10^{1}
^{95}Zr	Not discharged	3.93×10^{-1}	Not discharged	8.67×10^{-3}
^{99}Tc	Not discharged	1.30×10^{2}	Not discharged	2.86
^{106}Ru	3.24×10^{-2}	1.96×10^{4}	7.15×10^{-4}	4.33×10^{2}
^{125}Sb	Not discharged	1.34×10^{3}	Not discharged	2.96×10^{1}
^{129}I	1.67×10^{1}	1.63×10^{3}	3.69×10^{-1}	3.60×10^{1}
^{131}I	1.18	Not discharged	2.60×10^{-2}	Not discharged
^{133}I	3.11×10^{-1}	Not discharged	6.86×10^{-3}	Not discharged
^{134}Cs	Not discharged	2.08×10^{2}	Not discharged	4.59
^{137}Cs	5.96×10^{-5}	2.46×10^{3}	1.31×10^{-6}	5.43×10^{1}
^{144}Ce	Not discharged	2.94	Not discharged	6.49×10^{-2}
^{154}Eu	Not discharged	4.09	Not discharged	9.02×10^{-2}
^{234}U	Not discharged	6.19	Not discharged	1.37×10^{-1}
^{238}Pu	7.46×10^{-6}	9.38	1.65×10^{-7}	2.07×10^{-1}
^{239}Pu	5.99×10^{-6}	4.97	1.32×10^{-7}	1.10×10^{-1}
^{241}Pu	Not discharged	2.09×10^{2}	Not discharged	4.61
^{241}Am	Not discharged	5.70	Not discharged	1.26×10^{-1}
^{244}Cm	Not discharged	2.45	Not discharged	5.40×10^{-2}

Table B5. General modelling data

General model data	
Meteorological file	**60% Category D**
Effective stack / release height	**Height (m)**
Mill tailings	10 rising to 30
Enrichment and fabrication	30
Power production	30
Reprocessing	30
Collective dose population	
Mill tailings (out to a distance of 2 000 km)	1 person/km^2
Enrichment and fabrication	Europe
Power production	Europe
Reprocessing	Europe

Table B6. Critical group intake data

Food, drinking water and inhalation rates	Annual consumption rates (kg/a)	
	Infants	**Adults**
Milk + Milk products	200	200
Meat + Meat products	10	75
Green vegetables	20	40
Root vegetables	50	60
Cereals	30	110
Fruit + Fruit juice	50	60
Freshwater fish	1*	10
Sea fish	5*	100*
Crustaceans	0*	20*
Molluscs	0*	20*
Drinking water	250	440
	Inhalation rate (m^3/a)	
Inhalation rate (m^3/a)	1 900	7 300

*   Data taken from NRPB-M636, remaining data provided by Germany.

Table B7. **Occupancy data**

Occupancy data	Infants	Adults
Distance from discharge point (m)	1 000	1 000
Percentage of time outside (%)	10%	30%
River bank occupancy (h /a)	30	500
Beach occupancy (h /a)	30	2 000
Shielding afforded by habitation	Unitless	Unitless
Cloud γ	0.2	0.2
Deposited γ	0.1	0.1

Table B8. **Typical activity concentrations in freshwater bodies close to uranium mining facilities**

Radionuclide	Freshwater activity concentration (Bq L^{-1})
^{226}Ra	0.05
^{210}Pb	0.05
^{210}Po	0.05

Table B9. **Critical group doses in the 50th year
following 50 years of continuous gaseous discharges, from mill tailings**

Radionuclide	Annual Dose (μSv)					
	Adult			Infant		
	Inhalation	Cloud γ	Total	Inhalation	Cloud γ	Total
^{222}Rn	1.60×10^2	2.90×10^{-4}	1.60×10^2	1.60×10^2	1.80×10^{-4}	1.60×10^2

Table B10. **Critical group doses from the intake of contaminated drinking water
and freshwater fish in the vicinity of mill tailings**

Radionuclide	Annual dose (μSv)					
	Adult			Infant		
	Drinking water	Fish	Total	Drinking water	Fish	Total
^{226}Ra	6.16	7.0	13.2	12	2.4	14.4
^{210}Pb	15.2	104	119.2	45	54	99
^{210}Po	26.4	30	56.4	110	22	132
Total	**47.7**	**141**	**188.7**	**167**	**78.4**	**245.4**

Table B11. **Critical group doses in the 50th year following 50 years of continuous gaseous discharges, from fuel fabrication and enrichment – Adults**

	Annual dose (μSv)		
	Radionuclide		
	^{238}U	^{234}Th	Total
Inhalation	1.40E-01	2.50E-08	1.40E-01
Cloud γ	1.50E-08	1.90E-12	1.50E-08
Deposited γ	7.60E-04	0.00E+00	7.60E-04
Resuspension	2.20E-04	0.00E+00	2.20E-04
Cloud β	8.80E-13	8.80E-13	9.20E-13
Deposited β	0.00E+00	0.00E+00	0.00E+00
Green vegetables	2.00E-03	0.00E+00	2.00E-03
Grain	4.20E-04	0.00E+00	4.20E-04
Root vegetables	8.00E-05	0.00E+00	8.00E-05
Cow meat	2.60E-04	2.60E-04	2.60E-04
Milk	2.10E-03	0.00E+00	2.10E-03
Fruit	1.20E-03	0.00E+00	1.20E-03
Total	**1.50E-01**	**2.50E-08**	**1.50E-01**

Table B12. **Critical group doses in the 50th year following 50 years of continuous gaseous discharges, from fuel fabrication and enrichment – Infants**

	Annual dose (μSv)		
	Radionuclide		
	^{238}U	^{234}Th	Total
Inhalation	1.20E-01	2.60E-08	1.20E-01
Cloud γ	9.60E-09	1.20E-12	9.60E-09
Deposited γ	3.90E-04	0.00E+00	3.90E-04
Resuspension	1.80E-04	0.00E+00	1.80E-04
Cloud β	8.80E-13	3.50E-14	9.20E-13
Deposited β	0.00E+00	0.00E+00	0.00E+00
Green vegetables	2.60E-03	0.00E+00	2.60E-03
Grain	2.60E-03	0.00E+00	3.00E-04
Root vegetables	1.80E-04	0.00E+00	1.80E-04
Cow meat	9.20E-05	0.00E+00	9.20E-05
Milk	5.60E-03	0.00E+00	5.60E-03
Fruit	5.60E-03	0.00E+00	2.70E-03
Total	**1.30E-01**	**2.60E-08**	**1.30E-01**

Table B13. **Critical group doses in the 50th year following 50 years of continuous liquid discharges, from fuel fabrication and enrichment – Adults**

Radionuclide	Annual dose (µSv)						
	Fish	Crustaceans	Molluscs	Gamma	Beta	Sea spray	Total
^{230}Th	3.70E-01	1.20E-01	1.20E-01	1.60E-02	0.00E+00	3.50E-07	**6.40E-01**
^{232}Th	1.10E-02	3.70E-03	3.70E-03	3.60E-04	0.00E+00	1.70E-08	**1.90E-02**
^{234}Th	1.07E+01	3.60E+00	3.60E+00	3.00E+00	0.00E+00	3.53E-07	**2.09E+01**
^{234}U	5.70E-02	1.10E-01	3.40E-01	3.20E-03	0.00E+00	6.60E-07	**5.20E-01**
Total	**1.11E+01**	**3.80E+00**	**4.10E+00**	**3.02E+00**	**0.00E+00**	**1.40E-06**	**2.20E+01**

Table B14. **Critical group doses in the 50th year following 50 years of continuous liquid discharges, from fuel fabrication and enrichment – Infants**

Radionuclide	Annual dose (µSv)						
	Fish	Crustaceans	Molluscs	Gamma	Beta	Sea spray	Total
^{230}Th	3.60E-02	0.00E+00	0.00E+00	2.30E-04	0.00E+00	3.40E-09	**3.70E-02**
^{232}Th	1.10E-03	0.00E+00	0.00E+00	5.40E-06	0.00E+00	1.30E-10	**1.10E-03**
^{234}Th	4.07E+00	0.00E+00	0.00E+00	4.49E-02	0.00E+00	5.56E-09	**4.11E+00**
^{234}U	7.50E-03	0.00E+00	0.00E+00	4.80E-05	0.00E+00	8.10E-09	**7.60E-03**
Total	**4.11E+00**	**0.00E+00**	**0.00E+00**	**4.52E-02**	**0.00E+00**	**1.70E-08**	**4.15E+00**

Table B15.   Critical group doses in the 50th year following 50 years of continuous gaseous discharges from a typical coastal PWR – Adults

Radio-nuclide	Annual dose (μSv)												
	Inhalation	Cloud γ	Deposited γ	Resus-pension	Cloud β	Deposited β	Green vegetables	Grain	Root vegetables	Cow meat	Milk	Fruit	Total
^{3}H	2.80E-03	0.00E+00	0.00E+00	0.00E+00	0.00E+00	0.00E+00	4.40E-04	1.30E-04	1.20E-03	6.30E-04	4.40E-03	5.80E-04	**1.00E-02**
^{14}C	2.40E-02	0.00E+00	0.00E+00	0.00E+00	5.50E-07	0.00E+00	7.90E-03	2.00E-01	4.70E-02	4.40E-02	7.90E-02	2.40E-02	**4.20E-01**
^{41}Ar	0.00E+00	2.00E-04	0.00E+00	0.00E+00	3.10E-06	0.00E+00	0.00E+00	0.00E+00	0.00E+00	0.00E+00	0.00E+00	0.00E+00	**2.00E-04**
^{58}Co	2.40E-08	7.80E-10	1.90E-07	1.50E-11	1.10E-14	2.80E-10	4.10E-09	3.50E-09	3.40E-11	5.70E-10	2.30E-08	1.10E-09	**2.40E-07**
^{60}Co	5.60E-09	7.50E-11	3.40E-07	6.40E-12	1.00E-13	0.00E+00	9.00E-10	1.40E-09	1.20E-10	4.30E-10	5.50E-09	5.20E-10	**3.50E-07**
^{85}Kr	0.00E+00	7.00E-08	0.00E+00	0.00E+00	3.00E-07	0.00E+00	0.00E+00	0.00E+00	0.00E+00	0.00E+00	0.00E+00	0.00E+00	**3.70E-07**
^{88}Kr	0.00E+00	1.90E-06	0.00E+00	0.00E+00	1.60E-08	0.00E+00	0.00E+00	0.00E+00	0.00E+00	0.00E+00	0.00E+00	0.00E+00	**1.90E-06**
^{131}I	9.80E-06	2.90E-08	6.10E-06	2.10E-08	6.20E-10	2.60E-06	3.50E-05	5.50E-07	2.20E-05	3.30E-05	4.90E-04	3.90E-05	**6.40E-04**
^{133}I	2.60E-07	5.70E-09	1.40E-07	8.70E-11	1.70E-10	2.20E-06	1.30E-07	4.40E-29	3.00E-09	8.90E-09	8.00E-07	1.70E-07	**3.70E-06**
^{133}Xe	0.00E+00	1.00E-06	0.00E+00	0.00E+00	9.60E-08	0.00E+00	0.00E+00	0.00E+00	0.00E+00	0.00E+00	0.00E+00	0.00E+00	**1.10E-06**
Total	**2.70E-02**	**2.00E-04**	**6.80E-06**	**2.10E-08**	**4.10E-06**	**4.80E-06**	**8.40E-03**	**2.00E-01**	**4.90E-02**	**4.50E-02**	**8.40E-02**	**2.40E-02**	**4.30E-01**

Table B16.   Critical group doses in the 50th year following 50 years of continuous gaseous discharges from a typical coastal PWR – Infants

Annual dose (μSv)

Radio-nuclide	Inhalation	Cloud γ	Deposited γ	Resus pension	Cloud β	Deposited β	Green vegetables	Grain	Root vegetables	Cow meat	Milk	Fruit	Total
^{3}H	2.00E-03	0.00E+00	0.00E+00	0.00E+00	0.00E+00	0.00E+00	5.80E-04	9.60E-05	2.60E-03	2.20E-04	1.20E-02	1.30E-03	**1.80E-02**
^{14}C	2.00E-02	0.00E+00	0.00E+00	0.00E+00	5.50E-07	0.00E+00	1.10E-02	1.50E-01	1.10E-01	1.60E-02	2.20E-01	5.50E-02	**5.80E-01**
^{41}Ar	0.00E+00	1.30E-04	0.00E+00	0.00E+00	3.10E-06	0.00E+00	0.00E+00	0.00E+00	0.00E+00	0.00E+00	0.00E+00	0.00E+00	**1.30E-04**
^{58}Co	2.50E-08	5.00E-10	9.70E-08	1.60E-11	1.10E-14	9.30E-11	1.20E-08	5.70E-09	1.70E-10	4.50E-10	1.40E-07	5.20E-09	**2.80E-07**
^{60}Co	5.00E-09	4.70E-11	1.70E-07	5.60E-12	1.00E-13	0.00E+00	3.60E-09	3.10E-09	7.90E-10	4.50E-10	4.40E-08	3.40E-09	**2.30E-07**
^{85}Kr	0.00E+00	4.40E-08	0.00E+00	0.00E+00	3.00E-07	0.00E+00	0.00E+00	0.00E+00	0.00E+00	0.00E+00	0.00E+00	0.00E+00	**3.50E-07**
^{88}Kr	0.00E+00	1.20E-06	0.00E+00	0.00E+00	1.60E-08	0.00E+00	0.00E+00	0.00E+00	0.00E+00	0.00E+00	0.00E+00	0.00E+00	**1.20E-06**
^{131}I	2.50E-05	1.80E-08	3.10E-06	5.30E-08	6.20E-10	8.50E-07	1.40E-04	1.20E-06	1.50E-04	3.60E-05	4.00E-03	2.70E-04	**4.60E-03**
^{133}I	8.00E-07	3.60E-09	7.30E-08	2.70E-10	1.70E-10	7.40E-07	6.70E-07	1.20E-28	2.50E-08	1.20E-08	8.20E-06	1.40E-06	**1.20E-05**
^{133}Xe	0.00E+00	6.40E-07	0.00E+00	0.00E+00	9.60E-08	0.00E+00	0.00E+00	0.00E+00	0.00E+00	0.00E+00	0.00E+00	0.00E+00	**7.40E-07**
Total	**2.20E-02**	**1.30E-04**	**3.50E-06**	**5.30E-08**	**4.10E-06**	**1.60E-06**	**1.20E-02**	**1.50E-01**	**1.10E-01**	**1.70E-02**	**2.30E-01**	**5.60E-02**	**6.00E-01**

Table B17. Critical group doses in the 50th year following 50 years of continuous gaseous discharges from a typical inland PWR – Adults

Radio-nuclide	Inhalation	Cloud γ	Deposited γ	Resus-pension	Cloud β	Deposited β	Green vegetables	Grain	Root vegetables	Cow meat	Milk	Fruit	Total
³H	2.00E-03	0.00E+00	0.00E+00	0.00E+00	0.00E+00	0.00E+00	5.80E-04	9.60E-05	2.60E-03	2.20E-04	1.20E-02	1.30E-03	**1.80E-02**
¹⁴C	2.00E-02	0.00E+00	0.00E+00	0.00E+00	5.50E-07	0.00E+00	1.10E-02	1.50E-01	1.10E-01	1.60E-02	2.20E-01	5.50E-02	**5.80E-01**
⁴¹Ar	0.00E+00	1.30E-04	0.00E+00	0.00E+00	3.10E-06	0.00E+00	0.00E+00	0.00E+00	0.00E+00	0.00E+00	0.00E+00	0.00E+00	**1.30E-04**
⁵⁸Co	2.50E-08	5.00E-10	9.70E-08	1.60E-11	1.10E-14	9.30E-11	1.20E-08	5.70E-09	1.70E-10	4.50E-10	1.40E-07	5.20E-09	**2.80E-07**
⁶⁰Co	5.00E-09	4.70E-11	1.70E-07	5.60E-12	1.00E-13	0.00E+00	3.60E-09	3.10E-09	7.90E-10	4.50E-10	4.40E-08	3.40E-09	**2.30E-07**
⁸⁵Kr	0.00E+00	4.40E-08	0.00E+00	0.00E+00	3.00E-07	0.00E+00	0.00E+00	0.00E+00	0.00E+00	0.00E+00	0.00E+00	0.00E+00	**3.50E-07**
⁸⁸Kr	0.00E+00	1.20E-06	0.00E+00	0.00E+00	1.60E-08	0.00E+00	0.00E+00	0.00E+00	0.00E+00	0.00E+00	0.00E+00	0.00E+00	**1.20E-06**
¹³¹I	2.50E-05	1.80E-08	3.10E-06	5.30E-08	6.20E-10	8.50E-07	1.40E-04	1.20E-06	1.50E-04	3.60E-05	4.00E-03	2.70E-04	**4.60E-03**
¹³³I	8.00E-07	3.60E-09	7.30E-08	2.70E-10	1.70E-10	7.40E-07	6.70E-07	1.20E-28	2.50E-08	1.20E-08	8.20E-06	1.40E-06	**1.20E-05**
¹³³Xe	0.00E+00	6.40E-07	0.00E+00	0.00E+00	9.60E-08	0.00E+00	0.00E+00	0.00E+00	0.00E+00	0.00E+00	0.00E+00	0.00E+00	**7.40E-07**
Total	**2.20E-02**	**1.30E-04**	**3.50E-06**	**5.30E-08**	**4.10E-06**	**1.60E-06**	**1.20E-02**	**1.50E-01**	**1.10E-01**	**1.70E-02**	**2.30E-01**	**5.60E-02**	**6.00E-01**

Annual dose (μSv)

Table B18. Critical group doses in the 50th year following 50 years of continuous gaseous discharges from a typical inland PWR – Infants

Annual dose (µSv)

Radio-nuclide	Inhalation	Cloud γ	Deposited γ	Resus-pension	Cloud β	Deposited β	Green vegetables	Grain	Root vegetables	Cow meat	Milk	Fruit	Total
^{3}H	2.00E-03	0.00E+00	0.00E+00	0.00E+00	0.00E+00	0.00E+00	5.80E-04	9.60E-05	2.60E-03	2.20E-04	1.20E-02	1.30E-03	**1.80E-02**
^{14}C	2.00E-02	0.00E+00	0.00E+00	0.00E+00	5.50E-07	0.00E+00	1.10E-02	1.50E-01	1.10E-01	1.60E-02	2.20E-01	5.50E-02	**5.80E-01**
^{41}Ar	0.00E+00	1.30E-04	0.00E+00	0.00E+00	3.10E-06	0.00E+00	0.00E+00	0.00E+00	0.00E+00	0.00E+00	0.00E+00	0.00E+00	**1.30E-04**
^{58}Co	2.50E-08	5.00E-10	9.70E-08	1.60E-11	1.10E-14	9.30E-11	1.20E-08	5.70E-09	1.70E-10	4.50E-10	1.40E-07	5.20E-09	**2.80E-07**
^{60}Co	5.00E-09	4.70E-11	1.70E-07	5.60E-12	1.00E-13	0.00E+00	3.60E-09	3.10E-09	7.90E-10	4.50E-10	4.40E-08	3.40E-09	**2.30E-07**
^{85}Kr	0.00E+00	4.40E-08	0.00E+00	0.00E+00	3.00E-07	0.00E+00	0.00E+00	0.00E+00	0.00E+00	0.00E+00	0.00E+00	0.00E+00	**3.50E-07**
^{88}Kr	0.00E+00	1.20E-06	0.00E+00	0.00E+00	1.60E-08	0.00E+00	0.00E+00	0.00E+00	0.00E+00	0.00E+00	0.00E+00	0.00E+00	**1.20E-06**
^{131}I	2.50E-05	1.80E-08	3.10E-06	5.30E-08	6.20E-10	8.50E-07	1.40E-04	1.20E-06	1.50E-04	3.60E-05	4.00E-03	2.70E-04	**4.60E-03**
^{133}I	8.00E-07	3.60E-09	7.30E-08	2.70E-10	1.70E-10	7.40E-07	6.70E-07	1.20E-28	2.50E-08	1.20E-08	8.20E-06	1.40E-06	**1.20E-05**
^{133}Xe	0.00E+00	6.40E-07	0.00E+00	0.00E+00	9.60E-08	0.00E+00	0.00E+00	0.00E+00	0.00E+00	0.00E+00	0.00E+00	0.00E+00	**7.40E-07**
Total	**2.20E-02**	**1.30E-04**	**3.50E-06**	**5.30E-08**	**4.10E-06**	**1.60E-06**	**1.20E-02**	**1.50E-01**	**1.10E-01**	**1.70E-02**	**2.30E-01**	**5.60E-02**	**6.00E-01**

Table B19.   Critical group doses in the 50th year following 50 years of continuous liquid discharges from a typical coastal PWR – Adults

Radionuclide	Annual dose (μSv)						
	Fish	Crustaceans	Molluscs	Gamma	Beta	Sea spray	Total
^{3}H	4.00E-04	8.10E-05	8.10E-05	0.00E+00	0.00E+00	8.60E-12	**5.60E-04**
^{14}C	2.40E-01	4.70E-02	4.70E-02	0.00E+00	0.00E+00	5.70E-13	**3.30E-01**
^{54}Mn	1.80E-06	4.40E-07	4.40E-06	3.40E-06	0.00E+00	5.90E-16	**1.00E-05**
^{58}Co	1.00E-04	1.00E-04	1.00E-04	2.10E-05	3.80E-09	1.40E-14	**3.30E-04**
^{60}Co	2.40E-04	2.40E-04	2.40E-04	6.30E-04	0.00E+00	4.40E-14	**1.30E-03**
^{63}Ni	3.80E-05	7.60E-06	1.50E-05	0.00E+00	0.00E+00	5.20E-15	**6.10E-05**
^{110m}Ag	1.60E-04	3.30E-04	6.50E-04	8.60E-07	1.60E-10	1.90E-14	**1.10E-03**
^{124}Sb	5.70E-05	1.10E-05	5.70E-06	6.80E-08	5.60E-10	7.80E-15	**7.40E-05**
^{131}I	2.30E-06	4.60E-07	4.60E-07	1.00E-10	6.90E-13	1.70E-15	**3.20E-06**
^{134}Cs	1.40E-04	8.40E-06	8.40E-06	2.70E-06	5.30E-09	1.10E-14	**1.60E-04**
^{137}Cs	2.80E-04	1.70E-05	1.70E-05	2.00E-05	7.00E-08	2.20E-14	**3.40E-04**
Total	**2.40E-01**	**4.80E-02**	**4.80E-02**	**6.80E-04**	**8.00E-08**	**9.30E-12**	**3.30E-01**

Table B20.   Critical group doses in the 50th year following 50 years of continuous liquid discharges from a typical coastal PWR – Infants

Radionuclide	Annual Dose (μSv)				
	Fish	Gamma	Beta	Sea spray	Total
^{3}H	5.40E-05	0.00E+00	0.00E+00	8.90E-14	**5.40E-05**
^{14}C	3.20E-02	0.00E+00	0.00E+00	7.00E-15	**3.20E-02**
^{54}Mn	3.80E-07	5.10E-08	0.00E+00	9.60E-18	**4.40E-07**
^{58}Co	3.10E-05	3.10E-07	5.70E-11	2.30E-16	**3.10E-05**
^{60}Co	9.40E-05	9.50E-06	0.00E+00	5.90E-16	**1.00E-04**
^{63}Ni	1.10E-05	0.00E+00	0.00E+00	8.00E-17	**1.10E-05**
^{110m}Ag	4.10E-05	1.30E-08	2.40E-12	2.70E-16	**4.10E-05**
^{124}Sb	1.80E-05	1.00E-09	8.40E-12	1.10E-16	**1.80E-05**
^{131}I	9.50E-07	1.60E-12	1.00E-14	6.30E-17	**9.50E-07**
^{134}Cs	5.90E-06	4.00E-08	7.90E-11	4.60E-17	**5.90E-06**
^{137}Cs	1.30E-05	3.00E-07	1.00E-09	1.00E-16	**1.30E-05**
Total	**3.30E-02**	**1.00E-05**	**1.20E-09**	**9.80E-14**	**3.30E-02**

Table B21. **Critical group doses in the 50th year following 50 years of continuous liquid discharges from a typical inland PWR – Adults**

Radionuclide	Annual dose (µSv)								
	Fresh water	Beef	FW fish	Green vegetables	Milk	Grain	Root vegetables	External	Total
^{3}H	8.74E-03	6.44E-04	1.79E-04	1.36E-04	3.44E-03	8.99E-04	3.64E-04	0.00E+00	**1.44E-02**
^{14}C	2.33E-04	1.34E-04	2.65E-02	3.17E-05	3.57E-04	3.89E-04	9.41E-05	0.00E+00	**2.77E-02**
^{54}Mn	1.09E-07	5.18E-08	2.49E-07	6.29E-09	1.66E-07	1.56E-08	1.42E-08	2.48E-07	**8.60E-07**
^{58}Co	3.96E-06	3.63E-08	2.70E-05	4.11E-08	3.87E-07	6.94E-08	4.20E-09	4.38E-07	**3.19E-05**
^{60}Co	8.24E-06	6.62E-07	5.62E-05	5.51E-07	7.06E-06	7.83E-07	1.40E-06	1.56E-04	**2.30E-04**
^{63}Ni	1.28E-06	3.56E-07	2.92E-06	1.39E-07	9.50E-07	3.69E-07	3.82E-07	0.00E+00	**6.40E-06**
^{110m}Ag	7.35E-06	6.17E-08	3.84E-07	6.05E-08	9.88E-06	1.10E-07	2.31E-08	1.51E-07	**1.80E-05**
^{124}Sb	3.42E-06	2.13E-08	7.78E-08	2.52E-08	1.14E-08	4.27E-08	1.35E-09	1.27E-08	**3.62E-06**
^{131}I	8.86E-06	1.09E-07	4.03E-06	7.60E-08	1.45E-06	8.03E-07	1.84E-07	1.07E-10	**1.55E-05**
^{134}Cs	2.84E-05	1.10E-05	1.29E-03	2.97E-07	9.77E-06	2.84E-06	7.48E-07	2.35E-06	**1.35E-03**
^{137}Cs	1.53E-05	8.74E-04	6.95E-04	2.47E-05	7.77E-04	9.74E-05	7.55E-05	6.72E-04	**3.23E-03**
Total	**9.05E-03**	**1.66E-03**	**2.87E-02**	**1.93E-04**	**4.60E-03**	**1.39E-03**	**5.36E-04**	**8.31E-04**	**4.70E-02**

Table B22. **Critical group doses in the 50th year following 50 years of continuous liquid discharges from a typical inland PWR – Infants**

Radionuclide	Annual dose (µSv)								
	Fresh water	Beef	FW fish	Green vegetables	Milk	Grain	Root vegetables	External	Total
^{3}H	1.32E-02	2.29E-04	4.77E-05	1.81E-04	9.17E-03	6.54E-04	8.08E-04	0.00E+00	**2.43E-02**
^{14}C	3.65E-04	4.92E-05	7.30E-03	4.38E-05	9.84E-04	2.93E-04	2.16E-04	0.00E+00	**9.25E-03**
^{54}Mn	2.72E-07	3.02E-08	1.09E-07	1.37E-08	7.24E-07	1.86E-08	5.15E-08	1.49E-08	**1.23E-06**
^{58}Co	1.34E-05	2.88E-08	1.60E-05	1.22E-07	2.30E-06	1.12E-07	2.08E-08	2.63E-08	**3.20E-05**
^{60}Co	3.72E-05	7.01E-07	4.46E-05	2.19E-06	5.60E-05	1.70E-06	9.27E-06	9.33E-06	**1.61E-04**
^{63}Ni	4.09E-06	2.66E-07	1.63E-06	3.89E-07	5.32E-06	5.64E-07	1.78E-06	0.00E+00	**1.40E-05**
^{110m}Ag	2.09E-05	4.12E-08	1.92E-07	1.51E-07	4.94E-05	1.50E-07	9.64E-08	9.06E-09	**7.09E-05**
^{124}Sb	1.24E-05	1.82E-08	4.98E-08	8.07E-08	7.27E-08	7.46E-08	7.20E-09	7.63E-10	**1.28E-05**
^{131}I	4.12E-05	1.19E-07	3.29E-06	3.11E-07	1.19E-05	1.79E-06	1.25E-06	6.43E-12	**5.98E-05**
^{134}Cs	1.36E-05	1.23E-06	1.09E-04	1.25E-07	8.23E-06	6.52E-07	5.25E-07	1.41E-07	**1.33E-04**
^{137}Cs	8.02E-06	1.08E-04	6.41E-05	1.14E-05	7.17E-04	2.45E-05	5.80E-05	4.03E-05	**1.03E-03**
Total	**1.38E-02**	**3.89E-04**	**7.59E-03**	**2.39E-04**	**1.10E-02**	**9.76E-04**	**1.09E-03**	**4.99E-05**	**3.51E-02**

Table B23. Critical group doses in the 50th year following 50 years of continuous gaseous discharges from a typical reprocessing plant – Adults

Radio-nuclide	Annual dose (μSv)												
	Inhalation	Cloud γ	Deposited γ	Resus-pension	Cloud β	Deposited β	Green vegetables	Grain	Root vegetables	Cow meat	Milk	Fruit	Total
^{3}H	2.40E-01	0.00E+00	0.00E+00	0.00E+00	0.00E+00	0.00E+00	7.30E-02	2.20E-02	9.70E-02	1.10E-01	3.70E-01	9.70E-02	1.00E+00
^{14}C	1.90E+00	0.00E+00	0.00E+00	0.00E+00	4.40E-05	0.00E+00	1.30E+00	3.10E+01	3.80E+00	7.00E+00	6.30E+00	3.80E+00	5.50E+01
^{85}Kr	0.00E+00	3.20E+00	0.00E+00	0.00E+00	1.40E+01	0.00E+00	0.00E+00	0.00E+00	0.00E+00	0.00E+00	0.00E+00	0.00E+00	1.70E+01
^{106}Ru	7.90E-05	3.20E-08	3.50E-05	6.90E-08	8.40E-09	2.20E-05	1.60E-05	2.40E-06	2.20E-07	4.80E-06	2.40E-08	2.10E-06	1.60E-04
^{129}I	5.10E-02	7.00E-07	1.90E-02	5.50E-04	3.80E-08	0.00E+00	1.70E+00	1.40E+01	2.50E+00	3.40E+00	1.30E+01	3.80E+00	3.90E+01
^{131}I	7.50E-04	2.20E-06	4.20E-04	1.60E-06	4.80E-08	1.90E-04	5.30E-03	8.40E-05	1.70E-03	5.00E-03	3.70E-02	5.90E-03	5.60E-02
^{133}I	4.00E-05	8.90E-07	2.00E-05	1.30E-08	2.60E-08	3.50E-04	4.10E-05	1.40E-26	4.60E-07	2.80E-06	1.20E-04	5.30E-05	6.30E-04
^{137}Cs	2.40E-08	1.60E-10	1.60E-06	3.30E-11	2.90E-12	2.90E-09	7.90E-08	7.80E-07	1.10E-07	9.40E-07	4.90E-07	6.20E-08	4.10E-06
^{238}Pu	3.00E-05	3.60E-15	1.40E-11	4.30E-08	8.70E-17	0.00E+00	1.30E-07	1.80E-08	2.20E-10	1.00E-08	4.80E-10	1.90E-08	3.00E-05
^{239}Pu	2.60E-05	2.40E-15	1.70E-11	3.90E-08	6.20E-15	0.00E+00	1.10E-07	1.60E-08	2.30E-10	9.00E-09	4.30E-10	1.70E-08	2.60E-05
Total	2.20E+00	3.20E+00	2.00E-02	5.50E-04	1.40E+01	5.60E-04	3.10E+00	4.50E+01	6.30E+00	1.00E+01	2.00E+01	7.70E+00	1.10E+02

Table B24. Critical group doses in the 50th year following 50 years of continuous gaseous discharges from a typical reprocessing plant – Infants

Annual dose (µSv)

Radio-nuclide	Inhalation	Cloud γ	Deposited γ	Resus-pension	Cloud β	Deposited β	Green vegetables	Grain	Root vegetables	Cow meat	Milk	Fruit	Total
³H	1.60E-01	0.00E+00	0.00E+00	0.00E+00	0.00E+00	0.00E+00	9.80E-02	1.60E-02	2.20E-01	3.80E-02	9.80E-01	2.20E-01	**1.70E+00**
¹⁴C	1.60E+00	0.00E+00	0.00E+00	0.00E+00	4.40E-05	0.00E+00	1.70E+00	2.30E+01	8.60E+00	2.60E+00	1.70E+01	8.60E+00	**6.40E+01**
⁸⁵Kr	0.00E+00	2.00E+00	0.00E+00	0.00E+00	1.40E+01	0.00E+00	0.00E+00	0.00E+00	0.00E+00	0.00E+00	0.00E+00	0.00E+00	**1.60E+01**
¹⁰⁶Ru	8.00E-05	2.00E-08	1.80E-05	7.10E-08	8.40E-09	7.50E-06	5.70E-05	4.60E-06	1.30E-06	4.50E-06	1.70E-07	1.20E-05	**1.90E-04**
¹²⁹I	3.20E-02	4.40E-07	9.90E-03	3.40E-04	3.80E-08	0.00E+00	1.70E+00	7.60E+00	4.10E+00	8.90E-01	2.70E+01	6.30E+00	**4.70E+01**
¹³¹I	1.90E-03	1.40E-06	2.20E-04	4.00E-06	4.80E-08	6.50E-05	2.20E-02	1.90E-04	1.10E-02	5.40E-03	3.00E-01	4.00E-02	**3.90E-01**
¹³³I	1.20E-04	5.70E-07	1.00E-05	4.20E-08	2.60E-08	1.20E-04	2.10E-04	3.80E-26	3.90E-06	3.80E-06	1.30E-03	4.50E-04	**2.20E-03**
¹³⁷Cs	7.20E-09	1.00E-10	8.30E-07	1.00E-11	2.90E-12	9.80E-10	3.70E-08	2.00E-07	8.50E-08	1.20E-07	4.50E-07	4.70E-08	**1.80E-06**
²³⁸Pu	1.20E-05	2.30E-15	7.00E-12	1.80E-08	8.70E-17	0.00E+00	1.10E-07	8.60E-09	3.20E-10	2.30E-09	8.30E-10	2.70E-08	**1.30E-05**
²³⁹Pu	1.00E-05	1.60E-15	8.90E-12	1.60E-08	6.20E-15	0.00E+00	9.30E-08	7.30E-09	3.30E-10	2.00E-09	7.30E-10	2.40E-08	**1.10E-05**
Total	**1.80E+00**	**2.00E+00**	**1.00E-02**	**3.50E-04**	**1.40E+01**	**1.90E-04**	**3.60E+00**	**3.10E+01**	**1.30E+01**	**3.50E+00**	**4.50E+01**	**1.50E+01**	**1.30E+02**

Table B25. Critical group doses in the 50th year following 50 years of continuous liquid discharges from a typical reprocessing plant – Adults

Radionuclide	Annual dose (μSv)						
	Fish	Crustaceans	Molluscs	Gamma	Beta	Sea spray	Total
^{3}H	2.70E-01	5.50E-02	5.50E-02	0.00E+00	0.00E+00	5.80E-09	**3.80E-01**
^{14}C	1.40E+02	2.80E+01	2.80E+01	0.00E+00	0.00E+00	3.40E-10	**2.00E+02**
^{54}Mn	5.60E-03	1.40E-03	1.40E-02	1.10E-02	0.00E+00	1.90E-12	**3.20E-02**
^{57}Co	1.20E-04	1.20E-04	1.20E-04	4.10E-05	0.00E+00	2.00E-14	**4.00E-04**
^{58}Co	4.70E-03	4.70E-03	4.70E-03	9.40E-04	1.70E-07	6.40E-13	**1.50E-02**
^{60}Co	7.00E-01	7.00E-01	7.00E-01	1.90E+00	0.00E+00	1.30E-10	**4.00E+00**
^{63}Ni	1.20E-02	2.50E-03	5.00E-03	0.00E+00	0.00E+00	1.70E-12	**2.00E-02**
^{65}Zn	6.70E-03	6.70E-02	4.00E-02	5.30E-05	0.00E+00	7.10E-14	**1.10E-01**
^{89}Sr	2.20E-04	4.30E-05	2.20E-05	1.90E-09	6.60E-07	5.40E-12	**2.80E-04**
^{90}Sr-	2.70E-01	5.30E-02	2.70E-02	4.10E-07	7.00E-04	3.70E-09	**3.50E-01**
^{95}Zr	7.70E-07	1.50E-06	3.80E-05	2.10E-05	3.80E-09	4.60E-14	**6.20E-05**
^{99}Tc	3.20E-03	2.10E-02	2.10E-02	0.00E+00	0.00E+00	1.40E-11	**4.60E-02**
^{106}Ru	3.40E-01	3.40E+00	6.90E+01	0.00E+00	2.30E-03	1.50E-08	**7.20E+01**
^{125}Sb	7.40E-01	1.50E-01	7.40E-02	7.30E-03	1.30E-05	1.70E-10	**9.70E-01**
^{129}I	2.30E+00	4.60E-01	4.60E-01	1.50E-04	0.00E+00	1.60E-09	**3.20E+00**
^{134}Cs	4.90E-01	2.90E-02	2.90E-02	9.20E-03	1.80E-05	3.70E-11	**5.50E-01**
^{137}Cs	4.00E+00	2.40E-01	2.40E-01	2.80E-01	9.80E-04	3.10E-10	**4.70E+00**
^{144}Ce	4.50E-05	1.80E-04	8.90E-04	5.50E-05	0.00E+00	2.80E-12	**1.20E-03**
^{154}Eu	5.20E-04	3.50E-04	2.40E-03	1.50E-02	7.80E-05	5.80E-12	**1.80E-02**
^{234}U	3.90E-04	7.70E-04	2.30E-03	1.10E-06	0.00E+00	3.80E-09	**3.50E-03**
^{238}Pu	5.50E-02	8.30E-02	8.30E-01	8.00E-05	0.00E+00	1.20E-08	**9.60E-01**
^{239}Pu	3.20E-02	4.80E-02	4.80E-01	2.00E-05	0.00E+00	6.80E-09	**5.60E-01**
^{241}Pu	2.60E-02	3.80E-02	3.80E-01	3.10E-06	0.00E+00	5.10E-09	**4.50E-01**
^{241}Am	3.40E-03	6.90E-03	2.80E-01	1.90E-03	0.00E+00	6.50E-09	**2.90E-01**
^{244}Cm	8.80E-04	1.80E-03	1.10E-01	2.50E-05	0.00E+00	1.80E-09	**1.10E-01**
Total	**1.50E+02**	**3.40E+01**	**1.00E+02**	**2.20E+00**	**4.10E-03**	**6.20E-08**	**2.90E+02**

Table B26. **Critical group doses in the 50th year following 50 year
of continuous liquid discharges from a typical reprocessing plant – Infants**

Radionuclide	Annual dose at 50 years (μSv)						
	Fish	**Crustaceans**	**Molluscs**	**Gamma**	**Beta**	**Sea spray**	**Total**
^{3}H	3.70E-02	0.00E+00	0.00E+00	0.00E+00	0.00E+00	6.10E-11	**3.70E-02**
^{14}C	1.90E+01	0.00E+00	0.00E+00	0.00E+00	0.00E+00	4.20E-12	**1.90E+01**
^{54}Mn	1.20E-03	0.00E+00	0.00E+00	1.60E-04	0.00E+00	3.10E-14	**1.40E-03**
^{57}Co	4.50E-05	0.00E+00	0.00E+00	6.10E-07	0.00E+00	3.10E-16	**4.60E-05**
^{58}Co	1.40E-03	0.00E+00	0.00E+00	1.40E-05	2.60E-09	1.00E-14	**1.40E-03**
^{60}Co	2.80E-01	0.00E+00	0.00E+00	2.80E-02	0.00E+00	1.70E-12	**3.00E-01**
^{63}Ni	3.50E-03	0.00E+00	0.00E+00	0.00E+00	0.00E+00	2.60E-14	**3.50E-03**
^{65}Zn	1.40E-03	0.00E+00	0.00E+00	7.90E-07	0.00E+00	1.10E-15	**1.40E-03**
^{89}Sr	7.50E-05	0.00E+00	0.00E+00	2.90E-11	9.90E-09	8.30E-14	**7.50E-05**
^{90}Sr	3.50E-02	0.00E+00	0.00E+00	6.10E-09	1.00E-05	4.40E-11	**3.50E-02**
^{95}Zr	2.30E-07	0.00E+00	0.00E+00	3.10E-07	5.60E-11	6.00E-16	**5.40E-07**
^{99}Tc	1.20E-03	0.00E+00	0.00E+00	0.00E+00	0.00E+00	1.80E-13	**1.20E-03**
^{106}Ru	1.20E-01	0.00E+00	0.00E+00	0.00E+00	3.40E-05	2.30E-10	**1.20E-01**
^{125}Sb	2.10E-01	0.00E+00	0.00E+00	1.10E-04	1.90E-07	2.30E-12	**2.10E-01**
^{129}I	2.30E-01	0.00E+00	0.00E+00	2.20E-06	0.00E+00	1.50E-11	**2.30E-01**
^{134}Cs	2.00E-02	0.00E+00	0.00E+00	1.40E-04	2.70E-07	1.60E-13	**2.10E-02**
^{137}Cs	1.80E-01	0.00E+00	0.00E+00	4.30E-03	1.50E-05	1.40E-12	**1.90E-01**
^{144}Ce	1.70E-05	0.00E+00	0.00E+00	8.20E-07	0.00E+00	4.80E-14	**1.80E-05**
^{154}Eu	1.60E-04	0.00E+00	0.00E+00	2.20E-04	1.20E-06	6.40E-14	**3.80E-04**
^{234}U	5.10E-05	0.00E+00	0.00E+00	1.60E-08	0.00E+00	4.60E-11	**5.10E-05**
^{238}Pu	4.80E-03	0.00E+00	0.00E+00	1.20E-06	0.00E+00	7.40E-11	**4.80E-03**
^{239}Pu	2.70E-03	0.00E+00	0.00E+00	3.00E-07	0.00E+00	4.10E-11	**2.70E-03**
^{241}Pu	1.50E-03	0.00E+00	0.00E+00	4.70E-08	0.00E+00	2.10E-11	**1.50E-03**
^{241}Am	3.20E-04	0.00E+00	0.00E+00	2.80E-05	0.00E+00	4.10E-11	**3.50E-04**
^{244}Cm	1.10E-04	0.00E+00	0.00E+00	3.70E-07	0.00E+00	1.50E-11	**1.10E-04**
Total	**2.10E+01**	**0.00E+00**	**0.00E+00**	**3.30E-02**	**6.10E-05**	**5.90E-10**	**2.10E+01**

Table B27. **Collective doses from mill tailings normalised to gigawatt-years generated
truncated at 500 years (Population density 1 person / km^2)**

Radionuclide	Collective dose (manSv)						
	0-100 km			100-2 000km			**Grand total**
	Cloud γ	Inhalation	Total	Cloud γ	Inhalation	Total	
^{222}Rn	9.70E-09	1.20E-03	1.20E-3	9.40E-10	1.20E-04	1.20E-4	1.32E-2

Table B28. **Collective doses from mill tailings normalised to gigawatt-years generated truncated at 500 years: food chain pathways**

Radionuclide	Collective dose (manSv)
[210]Pb	2.13E-02
[210]Po	4.59E-02
Total	**6.72E-02**

Table B29. **Collective doses to the population of Europe truncated at 500 years following gaseous discharges from fuel fabrication and enrichment**

	Collective dose (manSv)	
	Radionuclide	
	[238]U	Total
Cloud γ	1.66E-10	1.66E-10
Cloud γ	4.86E-14	4.86E-14
Inhalation	5.43E-04	5.43E-04
Deposited γ	1.06E-05	1.06E-05
Deposited β	0.00E+00	0.00E+00
Resuspension	1.03E-06	1.03E-06
Green vegetables	6.57E-06	6.57E-06
Grain	2.20E-06	2.20E-06
Root vegetables	1.69E-06	1.69E-06
Cow meat	1.49E-07	1.49E-07
Cow liver	5.43E-09	5.43E-09
Sheep meat	6.57E-08	6.57E-08
Sheep liver	3.43E-09	3.43E-09
Milk	6.29E-06	6.29E-06
Milk products	6.57E-05	6.57E-05
Total	**6.29E-04**	**6.29E-04**

Table B30. **Collective doses to the population of Europe truncated at 500 years following liquid releases from fuel fabrication and enrichment**

Radionuclide	Collective dose (manSv)
[230]Th	1.30E-05
[232]Th	3.70E-07
[234]Th	2.50E-04
[234]U	1.80E-05
Total	2.80E-04

Table B31.   Collective doses to the population of Europe truncated at 500 years following gaseous discharges from a typical coastal PWR (Normalised to gigawatt-years generated)

Radionuclide	Collective dose (manSv)							
	Cloud γ	Cloud β	Inhalation	Deposited γ	Deposited β	Resuspen-sion	Green vegetables	Grain
[3]H	0.00E+00	0.00E+00	4.95E-04	0.00E+00	0.00E+00	0.00E+00	1.96E-04	1.21E-04
[14]C	0.00E+00	9.35E-08	4.30E-03	0.00E+00	0.00E+00	0.00E+00	3.55E-03	1.78E-01
[41]Ar	1.78E-06	1.03E-08	0.00E+00	0.00E+00	0.00E+00	0.00E+00	0.00E+00	0.00E+00
[58]Co	1.59E-10	6.92E-16	1.50E-09	2.43E-08	4.49E-11	7.01E-13	4.49E-10	1.50E-10
[60]Co	1.59E-11	6.82E-15	3.64E-10	4.39E-08	0.00E+00	3.08E-13	1.12E-10	3.27E-10
[85]Kr	3.36E-08	5.33E-08	0.00E+00	0.00E+00	0.00E+00	0.00E+00	0.00E+00	0.00E+00
[88]Kr	2.71E-08	7.38E-11	0.00E+00	0.00E+00	0.00E+00	0.00E+00	0.00E+00	0.00E+00
[131]I	1.21E-09	8.79E-12	1.40E-07	2.34E-07	1.21E-07	2.90E-10	6.26E-07	6.45E-15
[133]I	1.68E-10	1.59E-12	2.43E-09	3.74E-09	7.10E-08	8.32E-13	5.70E-12	0.00E+00
[133]Xe	3.08E-07	1.21E-08	0.00E+00	0.00E+00	0.00E+00	0.00E+00	0.00E+00	0.00E+00
Total	2.15E-06	1.78E-07	4.77E-03	2.99E-07	1.87E-07	2.90E-10	3.74E-03	1.78E-01

Radionuclide	Collective dose (manSv)							
	Root vegetables	Cow meat	Cow liver	Sheep meat	Sheep liver	Milk	Milk products	Total
[3]H	6.07E-04	5.79E-05	1.59E-06	4.86E-06	2.71E-07	4.39E-04	2.06E-04	**2.15E-03**
					[3]H global circulation			**1.92E-05**
[14]C	2.52E-02	4.11E-03	1.12E-04	3.36E-04	1.96E-05	8.04E-03	5.14E-02	**2.80E-01**
					[14]C global circulation			**2.42E-01**
[41]Ar	0.00E+00	0.00E+00	0.00E+00	0.00E+00	0.00E+00	0.00E+00	0.00E+00	**1.78E-06**
[58]Co	1.78E-12	1.96E-11	4.86E-11	1.68E-12	9.35E-12	6.36E-10	4.49E-09	**3.18E-08**
[60]Co	1.50E-11	1.59E-11	3.93E-11	1.21E-12	6.64E-12	1.59E-10	2.62E-09	**4.77E-08**
[85]Kr	0.00E+00	0.00E+00	0.00E+00	0.00E+00	0.00E+00	0.00E+00	0.00E+00	**8.69E-08**
					[85]Kr global circulation			**1.07E-07**
[88]Kr	0.00E+00	0.00E+00	0.00E+00	0.00E+00	0.00E+00	0.00E+00	0.00E+00	**2.71E-08**
[131]I	2.99E-10	2.34E-07	7.10E-09	1.12E-08	7.38E-10	3.55E-06	3.36E-08	**4.95E-06**
[133]I	0.00E+00	1.78E-13	4.39E-14	3.18E-15	1.68E-15	1.03E-09	3.18E-40	**7.85E-08**
[133]Xe	0.00E+00	0.00E+00	0.00E+00	0.00E+00	0.00E+00	0.00E+00	0.00E+00	**3.18E-07**
Total	2.62E-02	4.21E-03	1.12E-04	3.46E-04	1.96E-05	8.50E-03	5.14E-02	**5.22E-01**

116

Table B32. Collective doses to the population of Europe truncated at 500 years following gaseous discharges from a typical inland PWR (Normalised to gigawatt-years generated)

Radionuclide	Collective dose (manSv)							
	Cloud γ	Cloud β	Inhalation	Deposited γ	Deposited β	Resuspension	Green vegetables	Grain
^{3}H	0.00E+00	0.00E+00	5.89E-04	0.00E+00	0.00E+00	0.00E+00	2.43E-04	1.87E-04
^{14}C	0.00E+00	1.12E-07	5.14E-03	0.00E+00	0.00E+00	0.00E+00	4.39E-03	2.90E-01
^{41}Ar	2.52E-06	1.31E-08	0.00E+00	0.00E+00	0.00E+00	0.00E+00	0.00E+00	0.00E+00
^{58}Co	2.06E-10	8.88E-16	1.96E-09	3.27E-08	5.98E-11	9.35E-13	7.01E-10	4.49E-10
^{60}Co	2.06E-11	8.69E-15	4.67E-10	5.89E-08	0.00E+00	4.11E-13	1.68E-10	1.03E-09
^{85}Kr	4.02E-08	6.36E-08	0.00E+00	0.00E+00	0.00E+00	0.00E+00	0.00E+00	0.00E+00
^{88}Kr	4.21E-08	1.12E-10	0.00E+00	0.00E+00	0.00E+00	0.00E+00	0.00E+00	0.00E+00
^{131}I	1.68E-09	1.12E-11	1.87E-07	3.08E-07	1.59E-07	3.93E-10	1.03E-06	2.90E-14
^{133}I	2.34E-10	2.15E-12	3.27E-09	5.14E-09	9.35E-08	1.12E-12	1.03E-11	0.00E+00
^{133}Xe	3.74E-07	1.50E-08	0.00E+00	0.00E+00	0.00E+00	0.00E+00	0.00E+00	0.00E+00
Total	2.99E-06	2.06E-07	5.70E-03	4.02E-07	2.62E-07	3.93E-10	4.67E-03	2.90E-01

Radionuclide	Collective dose (manSv)							
	Root vegetables	Cow meat	Cow liver	Sheep meat	Sheep liver	Milk	Milk products	Total
^{3}H	7.20E-04	6.17E-05	1.68E-06	4.77E-06	2.71E-07	4.67E-04	1.87E-04	**2.43E-03**
						^{3}H global circulation		**1.92E-05**
^{14}C	2.99E-02	4.30E-03	1.12E-04	3.36E-04	1.96E-05	8.50E-03	4.77E-02	**3.93E-01**
						^{14}C global circulation		**2.42E-01**
^{41}Ar	0.00E+00	0.00E+00	0.00E+00	0.00E+00	0.00E+00	0.00E+00	0.00E+00	**2.52E-06**
^{58}Co	2.43E-12	1.78E-11	4.30E-11	1.78E-12	9.35E-12	6.64E-10	3.08E-09	**3.93E-08**
^{60}Co	2.06E-11	1.40E-11	3.46E-11	1.31E-12	6.92E-12	1.68E-10	1.87E-09	**6.26E-08**
^{85}Kr	0.00E+00	0.00E+00	0.00E+00	0.00E+00	0.00E+00	0.00E+00	0.00E+00	**1.03E-07**
						^{85}Kr global circulation		**1.07E-07**
^{88}Kr	0.00E+00	0.00E+00	0.00E+00	0.00E+00	0.00E+00	0.00E+00	0.00E+00	**4.21E-08**
^{131}I	4.49E-10	1.78E-07	5.14E-09	1.12E-08	7.57E-10	3.55E-06	1.78E-08	**5.51E-06**
^{113}I	0.00E+00	1.12E-13	2.80E-14	3.36E-15	1.87E-15	9.35E-10	4.11E-41	**1.03E-07**
^{133}Xe	0.00E+00	0.00E+00	0.00E+00	0.00E+00	0.00E+00	0.00E+00	0.00E+00	**3.93E-07**
Total	3.08E-02	4.39E-03	1.21E-04	3.36E-04	1.96E-05	8.97E-03	4.77E-02	**6.35E-01**

Table B33.   **Collective doses to the population of Europe truncated at 500 years following liquid releases from a typical coastal PWR – Normalised to GWa generated**

Radionuclide	Collective dose (manSv)
^{3}H	9.35E-06
^{3}H global circulation	2.43E-05
^{14}C	7.94E-03
^{14}C global circulation	5.70E-03
^{54}Mn	1.50E-07
^{58}Co	2.99E-06
^{60}Co	1.50E-05
^{63}Ni-	1.31E-06
^{110m}Ag	1.40E-05
^{124}Sb	2.99E-07
^{131}I	4.95E-09
^{134}Cs	2.06E-06
^{137}Cs	5.89E-06
Total	**1.40E-02**

Table B34.   **Collective doses to the population of Europe truncated at 500 years following liquid releases from a typical inland PWR – Normalised to GWa generated**

Radionuclide	Collective dose (manSv)			
	Freshwater	Agriculture	Marine	Total
^{3}H	5.24E-03	1.57E-03	1.25E-05	6.83E-03
^{14}C	3.62E-04	8.79E-03	4.13E-03	1.33E-02
^{54}Mn	2.57E-08	4.33E-08	6.74E-09	7.58E-08
^{58}Co	1.09E-06	1.05E-07	8.20E-08	1.28E-06
^{60}Co	2.30E-06	3.35E-06	5.83E-06	1.15E-05
^{63}Ni	5.51E-07	1.06E-05	1.57E-07	1.13E-05
^{110m}Ag	4.37E-06	3.05E-06	6.81E-05	7.55E-05
^{124}Sb	1.98E-06	8.56E-08	8.03E-07	2.87E-06
^{131}I	4.49E-06	6.58E-07	3.21E-08	5.18E-06
^{134}Cs	2.50E-05	5.01E-06	5.97E-07	3.06E-05
^{137}Cs	4.87E-06	4.12E-04	2.06E-05	4.37E-04
Total	**5.65E-03**	**1.08E-02**	**4.24E-03**	**2.07E-02**

Table B35. **Collective doses to the population of Europe truncated at 500 years following gaseous discharges from a typical reprocessing plant – Normalised to GWa generated**

Radionuclide	Collective dose (manSv)							
	Cloud γ	Cloud β	Inhalation	Deposited γ	Deposited β	Resuspension	Green vegetables	Grain
^{3}H	0.00E+00	0.00E+00	9.93E-04	0.00E+00	0.00E+00	0.00E+00	3.75E-04	2.43E-04
^{14}C	0.00E+00	1.83E-07	7.94E-03	0.00E+00	0.00E+00	0.00E+00	6.62E-03	3.31E-01
^{85}Kr	3.75E-02	5.73E-02	0.00E+00	0.00E+00	0.00E+00	0.00E+00	0.00E+00	0.00E+00
^{106}Ru	1.50E-10	1.30E-11	1.21E-07	1.08E-07	8.61E-08	7.94E-11	2.21E-08	4.85E-09
^{129}I	5.30E-10	1.28E-11	1.77E-05	1.81E-05	0.00E+00	2.21E-07	1.26E-03	1.35E-02
^{131}I	2.20E-09	1.54E-11	2.42E-07	3.53E-07	2.07E-07	5.07E-10	1.08E-06	1.12E-14
^{133}I	6.18E-10	5.51E-12	8.60E-09	1.15E-08	2.43E-07	2.87E-12	1.96E-11	0.00E+00
^{137}Cs	7.69E-13	4.62E-15	3.74E-11	5.28E-09	1.12E-11	3.74E-14	1.12E-10	2.18E-09
^{238}Pu	1.26E-17	1.35E-19	4.64E-08	4.20E-14	0.00E+00	5.31E-11	1.75E-10	5.09E-11
^{239}Pu	9.70E-18	9.48E-18	3.97E-08	6.39E-14	0.00E+00	5.51E-11	1.52E-10	4.63E-11
Total	**3.75E-02**	**5.73E-02**	**8.95E-03**	**1.86E-05**	**5.36E-07**	**2.22E-07**	**8.25E-03**	**3.45E-01**

Radionuclide	Collective dose (manSv)							
	Root vegetables	Cow meat	Cow liver	Sheep meat	Sheep liver	Milk	Milk products	Total
^{3}H	1.21E-03	1.15E-04	3.09E-06	9.71E-06	5.52E-07	9.27E-04	3.97E-04	**4.28E-03**
							^{3}H global circulation	**3.82E-05**
^{14}C	4.63E-02	7.50E-03	2.07E-04	6.40E-04	3.53E-05	1.59E-02	9.49E-02	**5.11E-01**
							^{14}C global circulation	**4.50E-01**
^{85}Kr	0.00E+00	0.00E+00	0.00E+00	0.00E+00	0.00E+00	0.00E+00	0.00E+00	**9.84E-02**
							^{85}Kr global circulation	**1.20E-01**
^{106}Ru	5.52E-10	1.94E-09	4.85E-11	1.66E-10	8.83E-12	2.43E-11	2.21E-10	**3.46E-07**
^{129}I	3.31E-03	5.97E-04	1.39E-05	6.63E-05	3.31E-06	5.74E-03	6.41E-02	**8.66E-02**
							^{129}I global circulation	**2.52E-03**
^{131}I	5.29E-10	3.97E-07	1.19E-08	2.14E-08	1.37E-09	1.23E-05	5.73E-08	**1.47E-05**
^{133}I	0.00E+00	5.96E-13	1.50E-13	1.21E-14	6.40E-15	8.16E-09	1.17E-39	**2.72E-07**
^{137}Cs	3.30E-10	3.74E-10	9.67E-12	4.62E-11	2.42E-12	5.06E-10	5.49E-09	**1.44E-08**
^{238}Pu	1.28E-12	4.20E-12	1.26E-11	1.99E-13	7.52E-13	4.87E-13	5.31E-12	**4.68E-08**
^{239}Pu	2.20E-12	3.75E-12	1.15E-11	1.76E-13	6.61E-13	4.41E-13	4.85E-12	**3.99E-08**
Total	**5.09E-02**	**8.21E-03**	**2.24E-04**	**7.16E-04**	**3.92E-05**	**2.26E-02**	**1.59E-01**	**1.27E+00**

Table B36. Collective doses to the population of Europe truncated at 500 years, following liquid discharges from a typical reprocessing plant – Normalised to GWa generated from UO$_2$ fuel only

Radionuclide	Collective dose (manSv)
^{3}H	1.50E-04
^{3}H global circulation	3.96E-04
^{14}C	1.13E-01
^{14}C global circulation	8.17E-02
^{54}Mn	1.12E-05
^{57}Co	1.30E-07
^{58}Co	3.09E-06
^{60}Co	1.01E-03
^{63}Ni	1.03E-05
^{65}Zn	2.65E-05
^{89}Sr	2.43E-08
^{90}Sr	1.41E-04
^{95}Zr	2.43E-08
^{99}Tc	1.89E-05
^{106}Ru	3.09E-02
^{125}Sb	3.09E-04
^{129}I	1.86E-03
^{129}I global circulation	3.98E-04
^{134}Cs	1.70E-04
^{137}Cs	1.94E-03
^{144}Ce	9.93E-07
^{154}Eu	2.87E-06
^{234}U	1.79E-06
^{238}Pu	6.62E-04
^{239}Pu	4.21E-04
^{241}Pu	2.87E-04
^{241}Am	4.86E-04
^{244}Cm	1.45E-04
Total	**2.34E-01**

GLOSSARY AND CONVERSION FACTORS

Acronyms

AECB	Atomic Energy Control Board (Canada)
BWR	boiling-water reactor
HLW	high-level waste
IAEA	International Atomic Energy Agency
ICRP	International Commission on Radiological Protection
ILW	intermediate-level waste
LET	linear energy transfer
LLW	low-level waste
LWR	light-water reactor
MOX	mixed-oxide fuel
NEA	Nuclear Energy Agency
NPP	nuclear power plant
OSPAR	Oslo and Paris Commission
PWR	pressurised-water reactor
VTT	Technical Research Centre (Finland)
VVER	Russian-type design of pressurised reactor

Units

GWa	gigawatt-year
GWa(e)	gigawatt-year (electricity production)
GWd	gigawatt-day
GWh	gigawatt-hour
manSv	man-sievert
MW	megawatt
MW(e)	megawatt (electric)
ppm	part per million by weight
Sv	sievert
SWU	separative work unit
t	tonne (1 000 kg)
tHM	ton of heavy metal

pico	p	10^{-12}
nano	n	10^{-9}
micro	μ	10^{-6}
milli	m	10^{-3}
kilo	k	10^{3}
mega	M	10^{6}
giga	G	10^{9}
tera	T	10^{12}

Factors to be used for normalising to gigawatt-years generated

- *Uranium mining and milling*

Tailings for reference facility =	100 ha
Tailings for 1 GWa =	1 ha
Normalisation factor:	1/100

- *Conversion*

  Normalisation for uranium conversion: divide discharges in gigabecquerels per year by 35 to get gigabecquerels per gigawatt-year.

- *Reprocessing*

  Normalisation of discharges from Cogema's reprocessing plant assumptions:

  Reprocessing data for 1977

Throughput:	1 670 tHM	$\cong$ U
Assumed burnup:	30 GWd/tU	
Thermal efficiency of reference NPP:	0.33	(assumed)

  Hence the electricity produced by the fuel (1670 tHM) reprocessed in 1977: 45.75 GWa(e).

  Hence the normalisation factor of 45.75 applied on the collective occupational dose in 1997 (see Table 14, last line).

Scaling factors

- Scaling once-through/reprocessing option: 0.79 (141.7/179.3 t U natural = 0.79)

- In fuel fabrication occupational dose:

  Scaling for UO_2 + MOX fuel:
  $$[(0.0066 * 21.1) + (0.43 * 5.5)] / (21.1 + 5.5) = 2.504 / 26.6 = 0.094$$

  Scaling for burnup:
  40 GWd/t $\times$ 1/365 a/d = 0.1096 Gwa/t
  0.1096 GWa/t $\times$ 26.6 t = 2.915 GWa
  2.915 GWa $\times$ 0.33 = 0.962 GWa(e)

NEA Publications of General Interest

1998 Annual Report (1999)   *Available on Web.*

NEA Newsletter
ISSN 1016-5398   Yearly subscription: FF 240 US$ 45 DM 75 £ 26 ¥ 4 800

Radiation in Perspective – Applications, Risks and Protection (1997)
ISBN 92-64-15483-3   Price: FF 135 US$ 27 DM 40 £ 17 ¥ 2 850

Radioactive Waste Management Programmes in OECD/NEA Member Countries (1998)
ISBN 92-64-16033-7   Price: FF 195 US$ 33 DM 58 £ 20 ¥ 4 150

Radiation Protection

Methodologies for Assessing the Economic Consequences of Nuclear Reactor Accidents (2000)
ISBN 92-64-17658-6   Price: FF 200 US$ 31 DM 60 £ 19 ¥ 3 250

Monitoring and Data Management Strategies for Nuclear Emergencies (2000)
ISBN 92-64-17168-1   Price: FF 160 US$ 26 DM 48 £ 16 ¥ 2 850

Developments in Radiation Health Science and Their Impact on Radiation Protection
(1998)   *Free on request.*

INEX 2 – Second International Nuclear Emergency Exercise:
Final Report of the Swiss Regional Exercise (CD-ROM)
ISBN 92-64-06760-4   Price: FF 500 US$ 88 DM 149 £ 53 ¥ 11 600

ISOE – Occupational Exposures at Nuclear Power Plants – Eighth Annual Report
(1999)   *Free on request.*

Nuclear Emergency Data Management
ISBN 92-64-16037-X   Price: FF 480 US$ 79 DM 143 £ 49 ¥ 9 450

Order form on reverse side.

ORDER FORM

OECD Nuclear Energy Agency, 12 boulevard des Iles, F-92130 Issy-les-Moulineaux, France
Tel. 33 (0)1 45 24 10 15, Fax 33 (0)1 45 24 11 10, E-mail: nea@nea.fr**, Internet: http://www.nea.fr**

Qty	Title	ISBN	Price	Amount
			Postage fees*	
			Total	

*European Union: FF 15 – Other countries: FF 20

❑ Payment enclosed (cheque or money order payable to OECD Publications).

Charge my credit card   ❑ VISA   ❑ Mastercard   ❑ Eurocard   ❑ American Express

(N.B.: You will be charged in French francs).

Card No.	Expiration date	Signature
Name		
Address	Country	
Telephone	Fax	
E-mail		